THE POWER OF MENTORSHIP

FOR THE 21ST CENTURY

Don Boyer

Copyright ©2006 Real Life Teaching/Publishing

♦ Real Life Teaching/Publishing ♦
donboyer@realifeteaching.com

THE POWER OF MENTORSHIP
For the 21st Century
Published by Real Life Teaching/Publishing
donboyer@realifeteaching.com
562-789-1909
Whittier, California

Copyright © 2006 Real Life Teaching/Publishing
Library of Congress Control Number: 2006904097
ISBN- 978-1-4243-0424-0

All rights reserved. No part of this publication may be reproduced, stored in a retrieval system, or transmitted in any form or by any means without the written permission of the publisher.

Cover Design by Justin Spina
jspina@mediawestproductions.com

Editing, Composition, and Typography by Patti McKenna
Pcmckenna6@aol.com

Photos by Vics Magsaysay
vicsmag@yahoo.com

This book is available at quantity discounts for bulk purchase.
For more information contact:
Real Life Teaching/Publishing
donboyer@realifeteaching.com
Telephone: 562-789-1909
Whittier, California

Special Note: This edition of "The Power of Mentorship for the 21st Century" is designed to provide information and motivation to our readers. It is sold with the understanding, that the publisher is not engaged to render any type of psychological, legal, or any other kind of professional advice. The content of each article is the sole expression and opinion of its author, and not that necessarily of the publisher. No warranties or guarantees are expressed or implied by the publisher's choice to include any of the content in this volume. Neither the publisher nor the individual author(s) shall be liable for any physical, psychological, emotional, financial, or commercial damages, including but not limited to special, incidental, consequential or other damages. Our view and rights are the same: You are responsible for your own choices, actions, and results.

Printed in the United States of America

· Foreword ·

Charlie "Tremendous" Jones

No one can appreciate the power of a mentor more than myself because I was never privileged to have one. I did have many heroes and role models but never a personal mentor. You may be in the same situation. I have wondered many times what my life would have been like if I had a mentor like my friend, Fred Smith. Fred Smith was mentored by Maxey Jarman, a very successful businessman. Fred appreciated his mentor so much he waited until Maxey died to write his story in his book, "You and Your Network". I believe Fred's book reveals how a book mentor can be just as powerful as a personal mentor.

If you are privileged to have a personal mentor, that's great! But if you don't have one, a book you hold in your hands may be even better. I can say this with authority because all my mentors were great books. Frank Bettger, author of "How I Raised Myself From Failure to Success in Selling", was my first mentor when I was a young insurance salesman. Teaching a Sunday School class of eight-year-old boys, I relied on Henrietta Mears, "What the Bible is All About". She taught me to use humor and how to keep it simple. Later, I discovered Maxwell Maltz and "Psycho Cybernetics". Maxwell was also a mentor to John Wooden, and helped him become the greatest basketball coach in history. Some of my other mentors are Abraham Lincoln, Patrick Henry, George Patton, Winston Churchill, Norman Vincent Peale, Dale Carnegie, Napoleon Hill, Dorthea Brand, Booker T. Washington, George Washington Carver and many others.

I can say I owe everything I've accomplished in my life to my book mentors. Now you, too, will share the wisdom of some of the giants who will personally mentor you through the power of the printed word. As you read "The Power of Mentorship for the 21st Century", you will gain a wealth of information and advice from many masters of success, including my friends Don Boyer and Mel Brodsky. Don and the other magnificent authors in this book want you to share their vision. Let them mentor you toward immense personal and professional success.

Remember you only keep what you give, you only enjoy what you share, and you only find your life when you lose it. I've been a mentor to many, but I don't think I can compare the help I've given to the help they will receive from the books I've given.

I hope you will also do likewise.

Charles "Tremendous" Jones

Charlie "T" Jones, CPAE, RFC is a "Tremendous" Publisher-Motivator-Humorist. Visit his website at www.executivebooks.com or call 800-233-2665.

· Dedication ·

To all the Champions who have the courage to say YES! to their dreams, pursue their vision and leap forward in faith.

To those who do not quit when the going gets tough.

Last, but not least, I personally dedicate this book to every mentor, coach, teacher, trainer, and pastor; for without you, success would not be possible. Thank you for sharing your knowledge and your life.

· Acknowledgements ·

First and foremost, I want to thank my Lord and Savior Jesus Christ for giving me life and life more abundantly. His gift allows me to use my talent and skills to their fullest potential.

To my wife, Melinda Boyer, your faithfulness and commitment are priceless. I could never ask for a better wife; you are the best! Thank you for always being in my corner.

To all our children and grandchildren who give me the drive and staying power to act on my dreams so they may feel proud of their dad and grandpa for being faithful to his calling.

To all the authors in this book who were willing to step out in faith, to share their wisdom, experience, time and money to help make life better for all who read this book. I am truly humbled to be associated with each and every one of you. It is a privilege and honor to call you Friend. The faith, integrity and courage you displayed by co-authoring this book makes each of you a Champion of champions.

To Jim Rohn and Jim Rohn International for his contribution and granting us permission to reprint "Building a Successful Team". This article was submitted by Jim Rohn, who is America's Foremost Business Philosopher. If you would like to subscribe to the Free Jim Rohn Weekly E-zine, go to his website at www.jimrohn.com or send a blank email to subscribe@jimrohn.com. Copyright © 2005 Jim Rohn International. All rights reserved worldwide.

To Brian Tracy for his contribution and granting us permission to reprint "How to Write a Book". Brian is a renowned author of countless book and audio learning programs. To contact Brian or Brian Tracy International, go to www.briantracy.com.

To Zig Ziglar for his contribution and granting us permission to reprint "Affirmation Cards". To learn more about Zig Ziglar or Ziglar Training Systems, visit www.ziglartraining.com.

To Vic Johnson for his contribution and granting us permission to reprint "Can You Believe It". An accomplished speaker and author, Vic Johnson may be contacted via email at vic@asamanthinketh.net or go to www.AsAManThinketh.net.

To Charlie Tremendous Jones for his contribution and granting us permission to reprint "Books are My Favorite Mentors". Charlie, also known as Tremendous Jones, is the founder of Life Management Service and Executive Books. To contact Charlie and obtain more information, go to http://executivebooks.com/cjones.

To Patti McKenna, you are a blessing beyond words. Thank you for your gifts, talents, and dedication to this book. Your editorial skills are a masterpiece! You polished our writings and put a high-gloss finish on them. Thank you for making all of us authors looks so good.

To Justin Spina, thank you for using your gift and creativity in the design of this book cover. Once again, you've amazed me with your talent. Your contribution helped make our first book a big hit. The Power of Mentorship for the 21st Century cover is sure to score a Mega Hit! It was wonderful working with you.

To our readers and countless others who touch our lives every day, this book would not be possible without you. Please accept our utmost gratitude and heartfelt appreciation.

Contents

	Introduction	10
Chapter 1	Do You Know Where You're Going by Don Boyer	14
Chapter 2	Faith of the Dots by Ryan Blair	30
Chapter 3	If It's to Be, It's Up to Me by Jacqueline Sisson	36
Chapter 4	Building a Successful Team By Jim Rohn	42
Chapter 5	YGB: You've Gotta Believe by Hasnain Khaku	46
Chapter 6	How to Write a Book by Brian Tracy	54
Chapter 7	Welcome the Disciplines by Jerry Haines	60
Chapter 8	Principles of the Wealthy by Glen Curry	66
Chapter 9	Steps to the Top by Melinda Boyer	80
Chapter 10	It's Never Too Late to Make Your Life Great by Mel Brodsky	86
Chapter 11	Can You Believe It by Vic Johnson	94
Chapter 12	Happiness is a Choice by Matthew Kolling	102
Chapter 13	Brandslaughter by David Corbin	110
Chapter 14	What Goes Around Comes Around By Greg S. Reid	116
Chapter 15	Books are My Favorite Mentors by Charlie "T" Jones	120
Chapter 16	A Life Changing Procedure by Zig Ziglar	128
Chapter 17	If It Walks Like a Duck by George Ramirez	134
Chapter 18	Get Published Now by Andrew Chapman	140
Chapter 19	The Science of Success by Don Boyer a.k.a. The Professor	146

· Introduction ·

At this very moment in time, someone is becoming a self-made millionaire, someone else is driving away in the car of their dreams, another is marrying their soul mate, while still another is moving into a brand new dream home. I ask , "Why isn't this *you*"? and "Why not *right now*"? I know you have dreams and goals (or you would not be reading this book)! There is no reason or excuse why you cannot achieve them. If you are not living the life you want and do not possess the things you desire, the reason is twofold. Your own beliefs are holding you back, and you have not yet tapped into the power of mentorship. To put it another way, you simply have not yet said YES! to your dreams.

To have a dream and to say yes to a dream are two entirely different things. Because 97% of people believe these two things are the same, only 3% of all people embrace and achieve their lifelong dreams and ambitions. Within these pages you will find an expert team of coaches, trainers, leaders, and business professionals joining together for one purpose - to help you say YES! to your dreams. Locked within every human being is a champion yearning to be set free so he or she can fly. You have a purpose and mission in life, and as mentors it is our job to help you realize your purpose so you can fulfill it with passion.

The old saying "You can't take it with you when you die" is a big fat lie. Everyday, people take books, wealth, wisdom, inventions, songs, businesses, love, forgiveness, cures and untold fortunes with them to the grave...they remain locked inside, never shared and forever lost. Their special gifts are lost forever because they were never released during their life here on earth. Visit any cemetery and you will find a land abundant with real buried treasure!

People are always asking, "Why am I here?" You are here to release the unique gifts, talents, and beauty that God granted to you before you were born. True happiness comes from finding those gifts and then setting them free so they can bloom to their full potential. Right now, someone else is becoming wealthy from the exact same gifts and talents you possess! They have learned the secret of turning their passions into profits, and you can, too.

If there is one single message I want you to gain from this book, it is: *Now* is your time to succeed; it's your turn to shine; this is your big break, and you can have it all. Go to the mirror and look yourself in the eye and say, "Yeah, why not *me*? And why not *now*"? When you do that, you have taken the first step to saying YES! to your dreams and goals. There is a flip side to that coin. Every time you give in to discouragement, you're saying no to your dreams. Every time you quit or give up, you are saying no to your dreams. When you listen to negative people, negative circumstances, or even negative thoughts, you are saying...yep, you get it, you are saying no to your dreams.

The world said man can't fly. The Wright Brothers said Yes! to their dream.

Experts said that man can't run the mile in under four minutes...Roger Banister said Yes! to his dream.

The people said nothing can be made that will go faster than a horse and buggy...Henry Ford said Yes! to his dream.

The crowd said artificial light was impossible...Edison said Yes! to his dream.

The Kingdom said the world is flat - you can't sail that far, but Columbus said Yes! to his dream.

It does not matter who says no to your dreams and declares them impossible; what does matter is that you have the power to say YES!

Mentorship is a strong and mighty power. There is no better influence than to surround yourself with people who have achieved great success and to allow them to help bring forth your buried and hidden treasures.

What is your dream? What do you want to accomplish in your lifetime? What impact do you want to make in history? It is all possible – all you have to do is say YES!

The following is a sampling of the ways to say YES! to your dreams.

You Say YES! To Your Dreams By…

Mastering the Power of Goal Setting
Becoming Focus Driven
Increasing your Income
Starting your Own Business
Reaching Toward your Dreams
Finding your Purpose
Living with *Passion*
Investing in your Health
Developing Great Habits
Upgrading your Associations
Never Giving Up and *Always* Believing in Yourself

If you can think it, see it, visualize it, feel it, speak it, and believe it, you can achieve it. We are certain you can, and we are here to help you do just that. It's time to look up, because as Zig Ziglar wrote, "I'll see you at the Top"!

Don Boyer

Note: At the end of each chapter in this book, we share with you a short quote or motto you can use along the way. I call them "one last thought".

Don Boyer

Don Boyer is an outstanding speaker and prolific writer. His mission, passion and purpose are to help you reach your full potential. He is a proud father and grandfather and resides in Southern California with his wonderful wife, Melinda.

You can contact him at
donboyer@realifeteaching.com.

Chapter 1

Do You Know Where You Are Going?

Don Boyer

Have you ever gotten into your car and started driving without a clue where you were going? I hope you answered no, or at least not very often. Most of the time when we get in our vehicles, we know where we are going or have an idea of our destination. This is just common sense. Yet, thousands of people start their day with no clue or idea what they wish to accomplish, what they are doing, or where they are heading. Conducting your life without a guideline is the reason many people feel frustrated, confused, and accomplish very little.

You cannot plan your day, set goals, or be effective if you aren't aware of where you are going in life. For millions of people, their job and its daily routine dictate their actions and decisions. Why do you think so many are walking around their office like zombies? Unfortunately, they are working at jobs they hate, with people they can barley tolerate, and only making enough money to live from payday to payday.

Folks, there has to be a better way; and the good news is, there is a *much* better way. Please remember this; you don't have to work at a job you hate, doing things you don't like with people you can't stand. Yet, this is the plan that millions of Americans have based their lives on, and it may be the plan you are carrying out right now.

If this plan does not work (and we both know it doesn't), what is the answer? The answer is to find your purpose, flow with your passion, and learn how to turn that passion into a profit. This is the plan that most millionaires are following. To them, their work is not work, it is their passion, enjoyment, the love of their life; and they found a way to get rich from it.

No matter what your passion is, I assure you someone is becoming very wealthy and very happy by doing that very thing. My question is: Why not *you*? And, why not *now*?

There is only one thing that is holding you back…okay, maybe two. The first thing that is holding you back are your own personal limitations. The majority of our limitations are mental and self-imposed. Actually that is good news, because since they are self-imposed, they can be released.

The second thing holding you back is a lack of knowledge. This, too, is good news because I am going to give you the knowledge to find your purpose, live your passion, and turn that passion into profit.

Are you ready? Here we go!

The five things you must do in order to leave the workforce of misery, the encampment of lack, and join the ranks of the successful are:

1. **Know Where You Are Going**

    However, in order for you to know where you are going, you must first know what you want. How can you make plans if you do not know what you want in life? Here is a very easy way to find out what you really want in life. Ask yourself, **"What do I want that I currently don't have?"** Once you answer that question, write it down on paper and ask yourself that same question again; **"What do I want that I don't currently have?"** Continue asking yourself that question until you have a complete list of everything you really want but don't yet have.

    When you are done, you will have a list of what you want! Now that you know the things you desire, you must ask yourself if you are willing to pay the price tag to make that dream a reality. Only you can answer that question. What are the price tags of dreams? While each dream will have its own unique price, here are some of the cost factors that all dreams require to become a reality.

    > Commitment
    > Desire
    > Faith
    > Patience
    > Perseverance

Knowledge
Skill
Planning
Team work
Money

My millionaire mentors told me, "Don, if you are not going to complete a project or do it with utmost excellence…don't start it." This is great wisdom and advice. If you are not willing to pay the price to make your dream come true, find and pursue a different dream. There is a positive side to this, though. You will never be given a dream without the necessary ability to make it a reality. You see, dreams are seeds that are only planted where they can grow. When the dream is watered and nourished, it takes shape and allows you to possess it in a real manner or form.

In every acorn there is a forest. Your dreams in thought form are the seeds of your dreams in physical form. The dream is the seed, the price tag is the water, and you are the farmer. What do you want to do? How important is that dream to you, and are you willing to pay the price for it? If your answer is YES!, then that dream must stay on your list.

With the list of the things you desire in hand, it's now time to build a game plan to make those dreams come true. This leads us to the second thing you must do in order to leave the workforce of misery and enter the world of passion and profit.

2. **Find a Mentor**

Reading this book is a great start, but it is very important that you have mentors in two formats.

1) *Mentorship through curriculum.* Simply stated, you must set aside a certain amount of money and time each month for education, training, and development in the format of books, CD's, on-line training and live seminars. This type of mentorship is invaluable, for in reality you are gaining a wealth of wisdom, insight and experience from the world's greatest leaders at little or no cost! When you purchase a book or CD, you are simply paying a few dollars to cover the ink, paper, or plastic disk. The information is priceless and basically free - now, that's quite a deal!

Books, seminars, and audios hold tremendous power. They can help you change your life, improve your income, increase your successes, enjoy great health, and enable you to reach your goals and dreams. Never underestimate the power of mentorship through written or audio training. Every millionaire and successful professional constantly uses and benefits from this type of format.

2) *Personal Mentorship.* Finding a personal mentor to work with you is a fairly easy task. You should seek a mentor who already has what you want, or has already accomplished what you are attempting to do. You may ask, "Where do I find a mentor to help me?" If you are involved in network marketing, you will have no problem finding one. If you are in someone's organization, I promise you there will be a high-money earner who will be happy to mentor and help you.

If you are not involved in network marketing….get in! Get involved, not for the sake of the money, but for the invaluable training and mentorship it offers. For a few dollars, you can become involved in a reputable company; and the mentorship you will receive is outstanding. Who knows, network marketing may just be your ticket to wealth. It has created thousands of millionaires!

If network marketing is not your cup of tea, there are many great personal coaches and training programs available. I believe one of the best mentorship programs in the market today is the "The Millionaire Club", created by my good friend, Gregory Scott Reid, also known as "The Millionaire Mentor".

For a few dollars a month, The Millionaire Club will provide you with the information to guide you to the next level of success. For more information on this mentorship program, go to his website at www.Alwaysgood.com.

3. **Aim for Your Dreams**

This will take courage, all the courage you have, can muster up, and can borrow from your mentors. Millions of people have dreams, desires and goals; yet their reality seems so far away, they just give up. That is a sad story in itself, but it gets even worse. Not only do they fail to reach their dreams, they feel it is their mission to make sure you don't reach yours, either!

It takes courage to stand up to those who "in the name of love, and want the best for you" say you can't succeed, while circumstances, bills, obstacles, set-backs, and disappointments are all yelling "quit, give-up, it's too hard". Baby, you've got to fight, swing when you are going up, and swing when you are coming down, fight to keep going forward and fight when you are moving back wards. You must keep moving, ducking and weaving, and pick yourself up whenever you get knocked down. When it's all over and the dust settles, you'll find yourself on top.

Courage is not the absence of fear; it is taking action in spite of fear. Courage is what makes champions shine; it's what makes opposition finally retreat and concede. It is the force that raises you up and sets you on top. If you fall down, make a mistake, or if people laugh, courage says "So what?" and moves on toward the dream. Show me someone who only talks about their dreams, goals and inventions yet never manifests or acts on them, and I will show you someone who lacks courage. Skills and enhanced talent come from elements without, but courage…only comes from within. Will you dream of achievement or achieve your dream? Courage or the lack of it will provide the answer to that question.

4. **Purpose and Passion**

In 1968, I was eight-years old and living on the north side of El Monte, California. I remember walking down the street one day to the corner store, which was owned by good old Hank and Tootie. As I walked, I recall asking myself "who am I, and what am I doing here (on earth)?" It may seem strange for an eight-year old to be asking himself such profound questions. To tell you the truth, I'm not sure where those questions came from or why I was asking them at the time.

The one thing I do know is that it took me 35 years to find the answer to those two questions. Over that 35-year time period, those questions created many sleepless nights and many days of inner anguish. Failure to find the answers caused me to suffer professionally, financially, and in the ministry. Who am I? Why am I here? Those questions have echoed through eons of time. Mankind has been in search of their answers for centuries. Many books over the years have tried to address and answer those questions, only to leave man more confused than ever on this subject.

Little did I know that my mother had been giving me the answers to those two age-old questions since I was four years old. She would look at me before I got into bed at night and say "Now Donald, do you have to go **PP**?" PP stands for Purpose and Passion! Can you believe that? It took me 35 years of heartache and pain, yet I had the answer all along! When you understand your purpose, you will find that your passion is connected directly to it. Purpose and passion cannot be separated; they are interlocked.

I know you are asking "How do I find my purpose?" The first thing you must understand is that you were created **on purpose, with a purpose**. God gave you a unique DNA, and He put your unique purpose right into it. When you hit planet Earth, your purpose was already a part of you. There *is* a reason why you are here on this Earth at this moment in time. You were not designed to walk around like a man or woman lost in space…just existing. Heavens no! You possess greatness, and have been given a grand mission - you have a job. Job in this context means Joyous Overflowing Blessing. That is what you will experience when you operate in your purpose with passion.

Let's walk you through as you find your purpose. I want you to get pen and paper; and I want you to write down, as well as answer, the following three questions.

1. What am I good at?

2. What do I really enjoy doing?

Everyone is good at doing something; most are good at a number of things. It doesn't matter what those things are – write them down. Next, what do you enjoy doing? What brings you happiness? Is it shopping, cooking, reading, fishing, sports, exercise, or music? Determine what brings you joy, and jot that down on your paper. After you written those items down, take a few moments to really think about them……

Are you done? Good. Now, I want you to write down and answer the third and most important question. Pretend you had 10 million dollars in the bank. Now envision buying everything you've ever wished for and traveling everywhere you've ever wanted. After doing all of that and realizing you never again have to think about earning money for the rest of your life….**What would you do?**

When you can answer that question, you have found your purpose. If it is indeed your purpose, you will not have a problem experiencing excitement. In fact, your purpose should consume you with red-hot passion! Personally, if I had a billion dollars in my portfolio, I would be doing exactly what I am doing right now with my life - teaching, speaking and writing. That is my purpose, it is my passion.

You might say my passion is I love making pies, but how am I going to make pies all the time when I have a full-time job? Ask yourself why you love making pies. Do you love the aroma of a freshly baked pie, enjoy their flavor, or find delight in the joy you see in other people's faces when you share your pies?

Does that mean you should quit your job and open a pie store? Not necessarily, but the last time I checked, Marie Cavendar was making a fortune with those pies of hers. You have to dig deep inside yourself, and ask God how you can best use the gifts He gave you. It is remarkable that many people work at jobs they hate or can barely tolerate. The job they hate is *someone else's* purpose and passion. Yet more unimaginable is that there is a job out there that you would absolutely love, but someone else is doing that job and hating every minute of it. You see, it is your purpose and passion, not theirs.

My point is that regardless of what your passion is and what you like to do, someone in the world is doing it and getting rich from it. The big bear I had to wrestle down and put a diaper on was, "How do I make a living from my passion?" The answer I found was **"when your passion has a plan, your plan will support your passion".** What that means is you will have learned how to create a business plan, a plan of action that will turn your purpose and passion into a payday. Going from where you are to where you want to go takes planning, personal growth, mentoring, and guidance. After discovering their purpose and passion, rarely does anyone leave their current source of income and jump right in full time.

Many have tried to do just that, and it is a painful experience. Trust me - you do not want to take that path. The good new is, with time and proper planning, turning your passion into a payday is very doable and realistic. As my good friend Greg S. Reid, The Millionaire Mentor, says, "When you do what you love, and love what you do, you'll have success your whole life through." That saying epitomizes purpose and passion. Albert Einstein in his final days said, "There is no reason to live… without purpose." Don't die and leave this Earth without tapping into your purpose and living out your passion. I promise you one thing: If you make a commitment to find out what your purpose is and let your passion kick in, your joy, energy, spark, juice, and enjoyment in life will increase tenfold or more.

You will wake up in the morning with joy and a spring in your step. From the moment you awaken, your mind will be spinning and it will energize you throughout the day. The joy of living your purpose and passion will remain with you as you lie in bed at night and will be your usher as you drift into a sweet sleep. Yes, it will take some work and time to find your purpose and live your passion. It will take faith, courage, and a certain amount of risk to live out your dreams, goals and visions. But whatever investment you must make, whatever the price tag is that you must pay, always remember… it is worth it!

Someone once said, "If you don't live your life with enthusiasm, you will be fired with enthusiasm". Listen, one of the quickest ways to get a promotion and a raise is to incorporate enthusiasm into every part of your life. Then, the enthusiasm you display while you are at work won't be just a dance and pony show, it is the *real* you. Nobody wants to work around someone who is dull and looks like they are miserable.

I remember telling someone in my youth, "Wow if I felt as miserable as you look, I would commit suicide." I did not say that to be mean or rude, but even as a young boy I recognized that was no way to live.

When I was in school, there were some classes and subjects I hated; and those classes seemed to drag on forever. However, I always got through them by envisioning my goals, my dreams, and what I wanted to do in life. I did not get an 'A' in those subjects (come to think of it, I think I got a grade that matched the first letter in my name…Don), but it got me through times when I felt I would crack if the teacher said "Don, are you paying attention?" one more time!

You may have a job you hate, driving everyday in traffic, working for a boss who…well let's just say needs Jesus big time. It is during these times that you need to find your purpose and passion so you can start working on them part-time. This will give you the endurance to accept that what you are going through right now is just a temporary inconvenience, a mere pit stop on the path to living the life of your dreams. Life was meant to be experienced with zeal, zest, and vigor! However, if you don't understand and live your purpose and passion, it amounts to little more than a boring, stale, and dull existence.

5. Take Pride in your Workmanship

   Your workmanship is your signature, branding, and trade mark. Never allow yourself to produce inferior workmanship because you are bored or don't like your job. Poor workmanship is never an option. You will never advance to the next level of promotion unless your current and past workmanship is your very best. Not 'the' best, just *your* best.

   About 25 years ago, I was a janitor mopping floors, vacuuming carpets and cleaning dirty restrooms. It was not a glamorous job, but my uniform was always clean and pressed, the floors shined, and the restrooms sparkled. During my breaks and at lunch time, I would read success books and dream about becoming successful myself.

With pride in my workmanship and dedication to reading, what was the outcome? Well, today I drive a brand new Mercedes Benz, wear expensive suits, work from home, do what I love, (public speaking and being a published author), make a great income and am married to the women of my dreams…you tell me if you think this stuff works? When I shared this story with my wife, she looked at me and said, "I always wondered why you cleaned our house so well"!"

There you go, the five secrets that will lead you from the workforce of misery, to the joy of wealth. If I did it…so can *you*!

"Average people see things as they are...
Exceptional people see things
as they can be"

- Don Boyer -

Ryan Blair

Ryan Blair is one of America's most successful young entrepreneurs. Having been named to the Business Times' "40 Under Forty" list and featured as an expert on national television, print and radio, he speaks across the country as the CEO of PathConnect, a dynamic online social network where thousands connect with mentors each day for support in achieving their grandest goals.

Contact Ryan Blair at:
Email: ryan@pathconnect.com
Telephone: (800) 759-6839
Website: www.pathconnect.com or
www.ryanblair.com

Chapter 2

Faith of the Dots
Connecting My First 200 Memories

Ryan Blair

The universe is a masterpiece. It consists of billions of individual tiny dots which are purposely placed together to create a unique work of art. No dot is insignificant; each one is as vital as another in painting the universe. Every person in the universe is their own work of art. We are a work in progress; and every person, experience, memory and dream dot the canvas of our lives. Regardless of its shape, size, or color, each dot is there for a reason. They may seem like mere specks which are there for no apparent rhyme or reason, or they may be vivid stars, forming a very evident constellation.

Some people live their lives with no real purpose. They scatter from one dot to the next with no plan or goal. As I journey through life, my quest for its reason has led me to connect its dots in order to find my purpose. Although I've always had faith that eventually I would see the masterpiece, there were times when my life was a puzzle, much like a maze. A maze must be elevated in order to keep you from bouncing off its walls like a pinball machine. Our thought processes must also be elevated so that our star may shine and become a vital part of the constellation we leave behind.

Our memories are the dots of our past, and we lose our recall of them as they fade with time. Yet, these memories all produce the slide show of our lives. Thus far, the 28 years I have spent on earth have yielded 200 powerful memories. Since I do not have the capacity to vividly store many more, I am releasing those memories to make room for more.

My first one hundred memories, starting when I was three, were that of despair. My parents had been abused as children, and they despised the lifestyle in which they were raised. Unfortunately, they did not realize they were repeating the cycle and were abusive, as well. My earliest memories are of witnessing and later being the victim of the same abuse they had endured.

Although I was the youngest of six children, I was five years younger than my closest sibling. Therefore, I was frequently alone. At a young age, I developed a sense of survival. Later, I learned that I had a powerful gift for auditory processing. I was able to interpret pitch and tone; and I stored sounds and words in my mind's memory bank, withdrawing them as needed for my survival.

I have an older brother named Brian. His name is tonally the same as mine, Ryan. When my father became angry, I quickly learned how to determine which one of us was the focus of his anger before he got very close. In order to escape my father's punishments, I learned to set crafty traps to steer his anger toward

Brian. As a young boy, I had developed a rare identity and set of skills uncommon for a child my age.

It also became clear that I was different from my peers. A rebel in my youth, I was once considered the most dangerous juvenile in our county. Like Huck Finn, I found I could receive attention from my negative actions. I quickly learned the power of fear, so I used that power to stand out from the crowd. Fear was my double-edged sword. My parents used fear to suppress me, and in turn, I used fear to gain power over others.

By the age of 16, I was aware that these actions worked and could give me whatever I wanted. I was an overachiever in sports by this time; unfortunately, the rules of society required that I played those games in jail. My salvation actually came in the form of a meeting with a mentor, which was arranged by my mother. He had a different presence than most men I'd known; he had a non-threatening nature with a hint of femininity and refinement.

Later, my mentor rescued me and my mother. We moved from a rat-infested home in a high-crime neighborhood to his castle on an island, with exotic birds and a lake jumping with fish below my bedroom window. This peaceful and joyous environment brought me much pleasure. Elated, I now knew what I wanted in life, and developed a desire to learn everything I could in order to achieve a life rich with success.

My first hundred memories were now behind me, and I was free to create the second hundred. Traits which were previously dormant were awakened, and I developed ambition and a desire for accomplishment. Having only completed 9th grade, I pursued a rigorous course of study, completing high school within one year while simultaneously attending college. I spent the next two years with the curiosity of an infant, soaking up everything I could learn.

The next hundred memories read like a story tale. I surrounded myself with great thinkers and leaders. As their student, I learned what made them unique. My gift to them was the satisfaction they derived from contributing to others. In turn, they presented me with the gift of their knowledge and experience.

Not afraid to ask for help, I persuaded a major investor to fund my cause. As his protégé, this man challenged me and left me with no choice but to succeed. With his support and the wind at my back, I braved new territories. The lessons I learned from my mentors were invaluable to me, especially during times when success was not certain.

Driven toward my goal, I persistently moved forward with a "nothing can stop me now" attitude. With a clear mind and purpose, I drove on toward my master plan. It wasn't always easy, for I was often within a few short steps of major disaster or massive success. I persevered, learning that success requires determination and faith.

The culmination of those efforts was the realization of a new dream, using the knowledge I had gained about business and technology to create an online social network of success-minded individuals in search of mentors of their own. As a person of contribution, it fills me with pride to know that day after day, even those who don't hear my story are still connecting with mentors by the thousands.

Although I wasn't aware of it for some time, the ambition to succeed and contribute had been hibernating within me my whole life. Awakening that ambition gave me a new perspective on life. It gave me the opportunity to have experiences and create wonderful memories which few people are privileged to know. Those memories and experiences have become the dots on my canvas, and I tell my story to show you how those dots connect to paint my picture. The process of connecting our dots is designed to provide us with faith in our future. I share my memories not to impress you, but rather to impress upon you that life is merely a summary of actions taken, behaviors learned, and paths connected.

Through this, you have become connected to me by observing my dots or becoming one of them. Embrace the process, and you, too, will live a life of awe.

> *"Even leaders must look for support at every turn and not be afraid to ask for help."*
> *- Ryan Blair -*

Dr. Jacqueline Sisson

Dr. Jacqueline Sisson, A.T. is known as Dr. JAS "Heart Specialist". She is an ordained minister, has a Ph.D. in Psychology and is currently pursuing a Ph.D. in Homeopathic Nutrition. Dr. Sisson is a Business and Personal Coach for Jim Rohn International. Dr. Sisson has been involved on the cutting edge of the personal growth arena for over 25 years. A dynamic international speaker, she has what it takes to bring out the very best in the lives she touches. A Keynote, International Speaker, Personal Business Coach, she can be reached at: Office: (619) 691-1954 Fax: (619) 691-1951 Cell: (619) 993-4607.
Email: allthat772@aol.com
Website: www.atouchofhealthbyjacqueline.com

Chapter 3

IF IT'S TO BE, IT'S UP TO ME
The Power of One, It's ALL in YOU

Dr. Jacqueline Sisson

I believe that we are wonderfully created with a distinct purpose in mind. Are you fulfilling your purpose? Do you know what your purpose is? Look within your hopes, visions and dreams and you will find much of your own purpose. What interests and excites you? What are you most passionate about? What do you want to be or to do when you grow up? When dreaming, take care that your dream is your own and not superimposed by what others want you to be, to do, or to have. Design a life so huge that it will fit no one else but you. You alone are responsible for your actions or lack thereof.

What is the desire of your heart, your hope, your dream, your vision? Some of you may be proficient *"dreamers"*, while others are on the other end of the spectrum. This would mean that this is the first time you are seriously taking a look at your life's possibilities. No matter where you are on the scale, there is no better time than the present for you to design the life of your dreams. It is never too late. It is my desire that what you read here will inspire you on your journey of *creating* the *life* of *YOUR dreams*.

The power of one is all about YOU taking responsibility for your life, your beliefs, and your unbelief. Dare to look at the dream stealers of fear, unbelief, doubt, despair or "what-ifs" and say NO MORE. Make it clear that your dream stealers are no longer allowed to get in the way of blocking what you want in your life. No longer will they squander away your earnings; no longer will they keep you pinned to the ground.

It has been said, "I saw the enemy, and it was me". Don't allow that to be true in your life. Let others live in the arena of mediocrity, but not you - you belong soaring with eagles... Do you believe it? I do.

The Word of God says, "without a vision, (dream) we perish." which totally brings into perspective the importance of your Dream/Vision. A dream is very powerful. If you dare to take the time to dream, be sure and make it HUGE. What do you believe is possible? What do you desire? It is all within you, waiting to blossom. What *you* desire - bring into your life. Live each day to create it. Be aware of each choice you make, and ask yourself if these choices are bringing you closer to your dream. Dare to soar and dream of great things.

Three steps will help make your dream a reality. The amount of time you spend on each step will determine the degree of success that you will experience. First, *find the feeling*, then *create a visual*, and, lastly, *speak the vision into being*.

Find the Feeling - What is your dream? It can be as simple or as vast as you desire. The more detail you put into your dream, the more likely it will come to fruition. You do not want to rush through this step. While dreaming, take into consideration the many facets of your life. When I am creating my personal dream, I visit the major areas of my life. I check into my mental, physical, spiritual, relational and financial categories and explore the possibilities of growth in each one. I invite you to do the same. These categories can be found in each person's life and are the launching pads for dreams. Use as much detail as possible; begin to put pen to page and write about each aspect of your dream. Hold nothing back. As you write, can you see the picture, can you hear the sounds, smell the smells? Can you taste the flavor of success? The more detail you write down, the more invested you will be in making the dream come to pass.

Create a Visual - You have written your dream. Let us bring it to life through visualization. Purchase a large piece of paper such as "oak tag" or "poster board" in whatever color you desire. You will also need thumbtacks and some glue or scotch tape. These are the foundational pieces for your dream/vision board. Now begin to collect pictures, words, phrases, etc. that express and support your written dream. Accumulate any pictures of yourself or others who are living the life you desire. Don't question what you are drawn towards. If the picture resonates with you, clip it out and begin the process of "creating through pictures" the life you desire to live. The amount of time you spend on this is up to you. Invite your friends and family to save their magazines. Don't limit yourself to your personal subscriptions. You may find your own choice of interests too confining during this phase. After you have accumulated pictures, phrases, and/or words, it is time for you to lay out your paper and begin to place them accordingly. Enjoy the process and try each one out in different places on the page. Trust the process. You will know what picture is right and exactly where to put it. There is no right or wrong, simply go with the flow. You may use all or part of the pictures/words/phrases that you have collected. When you are satisfied with the placement of your layout, glue it down. Doing this activity uses the more creative part of the brain, while the former one of writing the dream uses a combination of the right and left brains. The more dimensions you use, the more solid your dream will be. Display your dream where you view it often. By "seeing" the vision, you are reinforcing your dream.

Speak the Vision into Being - There is a Scripture that says "speak those things that are not as though they were…". Review your dream/vision writings. Go through each of your categories, and ask yourself what you can do today to take the steps toward making the dream a reality. Begin to speak and live your life as if your dream/vision is a reality. Begin to live your life as if you already have the desires of your heart. Write affirmations as if you are living your dream/vision today. Keep them in present tense. For instance, if you want to be a speaker, join Toastmasters and state "I am a sought-after paid International Speaker." If you want to be debt free or have financial freedom, start being accountable today for your spending, know where your money goes and declare "I am debt free and live a life of financial abundance." If you desire to lose weight, be conscious of what goes into your body and assert "My body is at the peak of fitness." Learn to be a master of the gifts and talents that you possess.

A wise man once said… "Lord, I believe, now help mine unbelief…". Each facet of your dream is yours. It is my wish to "wish you more than enough" belief, vision and hope - that you join me in living the life of your dreams. Take steps every day to make your dream/vision become a reality. Grow each day in keeping the promises you make to yourself and to others. Whatever you say you are going to do - do it!

Only YOU stand in the way. Only YOU have the right and the responsibility to choose to act or not.

Remember - "If it is to be, it is up to me". Never underestimate the power of one.

"Use the pebble stone in your shoe
for a stepping stone to a greater,
more successful you"

- Dr. Jacqueline Sisson -

Jim Rohn

The following article was submitted by Jim Rohn, America's Foremost Business Philosopher. To subscribe to the Free Jim Rohn Weekly E-zine, go to www.jimrohn.com or send a blank email to subscribe@jimrohn.com. Copyright © 2005 Jim Rohn International. All rights reserved worldwide.

Chapter 4

Building a Successful Team

Jim Rohn

Once you've set a goal for yourself as a leader - whether it is to create your own enterprise, energize your organization, build a church, or excel in sports, etc. - the challenge is to find good people to help you accomplish that goal. Gathering a successful team of people is not only helpful, it's necessary.

So to guide you in this daunting task of picking the right people, I'm going to share with you a four-part checklist.

> **Number One:** Check each candidate's history. Seek out available information regarding the individual's qualifications to do the job. That's the most obvious step.
>
> **Number Two**: Check the person's interest level. If they are interested, they are probably a good prospect. Sometimes people can fake their interest; but if you've been a leader for a while, you will be a capable judge of whether somebody is merely pretending. Arrange face-to-face conversation, and try to gauge his or her sincerity to the best of your ability. You won't

hit the bull's-eye every time, but you can get pretty good at spotting what I call true interest.

Number Three: Check the prospect's responses. A response tells you a lot about someone's integrity, character, and skills. Listen for responses like these: "You want me to get there that early?" "You want me to stay that late?" "The break is only ten minutes?" "I'll have to work two evenings a week and Saturdays?" You can't ignore these clues. A person's responses are a good indication of his or her character and of how hard he or she will work. Our attitudes reflect our inner selves, so even if we can fool others for a while, eventually, our true selves will emerge.

And Number Four: Check results. The name of the game is results. How else can we effectively judge an individual's performance? The final judge must be results.

There are two types of results to look for. The first is activity results. Specific results are a reflection of an individual's productivity. Sometimes we don't ask for this type of result right away, but it's pretty easy to check activity. If you work for a sales organization and you've asked your new salesman, John, to make ten calls in the first week, it's simple to check his results on Friday. You say, "John, how many calls did you make?" John says, "Well . . ." and starts telling a story, making an excuse. You respond, "John, I just need a number from one to ten." If his results that first week are not good, it is a definite sign. You might try another week, but if that lack of precise activity continues, you'll soon realize that John isn't capable of becoming a member of your team.

The second area you need to monitor is productivity. The ultimate test of a quality team is measurable progress in a reasonable amount of time. And here's one of the skills of leadership: be up front with your team as to what you expect them to produce. Don't let the surprises come later.

When you're following this four-part checklist, your instincts obviously play a major role. And your instincts will improve every time you go through the process. Remember, building a good team will be one of your most challenging tasks as a leader. It will reap you multiple rewards for a long time to come.

To Your Success,

Jim Rohn

"*Attitude is greatly shaped by influence and association."*

- Jim Rohn -

Hasnain Khaku

Hasnain "Mr. Incredible" Khaku lives in Anaheim Hills, California with Tahera, his wife and inspiration in life. He is president of www.superstarsgroup.com and a top trainer for a NYSE company. He specializes in helping people start and develop their own businesses. For more articles on starting and succeeding in your business, contact him at: (714) 921-0606, email Hkhaku@aol.com, or visit his website at www.superstarsgroup.com.

Chapter 5

YGB®
(You've Gotta Believe)

Hasnain Khaku

It was a beautiful, sunny day in this third world city. The 17-year-old young man had just gotten the results of the most important and difficult test of his life. Not able to contain himself any longer, he looked over to his mentor, who was driving the car. The car windows were down, and the traffic noise was deafening. His mentor had a wide grin on his face. "I always knew you could do it... YOU'VE GOTTA BELIEVE", said the mentor to the young man. "Your mom and I are so proud of you. We will do whatever it takes to make your dreams come true."

The young man had just scored in the top one percent in the English Proficiency Test at the U.S. Consulate. Ever since he had announced his plans to go to America, his dad had been his biggest supporter. He helped him make plans, visit libraries, write to all the organizations and universities, and drove him everywhere he needed to go. Now, the young man was ready to go to America. The mentor was beaming with pride for his son.

Can you be a mentor to your own children? Absolutely! No matter what your economic or social status, "You've

Gotta Believe" you can! Chances are that you are already a mentor to your own kids and to other members of your family.

Mentors Help You Succeed

Mentoring is a very powerful life-changing force. The best thing that can happen to you is to be guided by the right people – successful leaders who will inspire you and fire up your imagination. They have vision. Mentors have the will and the ability to paint your future in a way that alone you never could.

Everyone looks at life through the filter of his or her own experiences. We place limitations on our lives based on our past performance. We measure our world by the things that have happened to us, or perhaps to our family. These so-called glass ceilings keep us from achieving our true capabilities. Good or bad, these are self-imposed limits.

Mentors help you overcome limitations and crystallize your vision. They remove these filters so you can view life more clearly.   Most of the time, your mentor believes in you more than you believe in yourself. Your mentors want to succeed. They help you say yes to your dreams.

You probably have mentors already, but didn't recognize their importance. Mentors come in different shapes and sizes. You may even have several mentors for different areas of your life. You can have a personal life mentor, a business life mentor, a spiritual life mentor and a mentor for every other aspect of your life. In fact, it is rare to find one person who can be your guide in all areas of your life. Even mentors have several mentors.

You can have mentors who are no longer alive, but they have impacted you by the way they lived their lives. We all have spiritual leaders from the past who have made an amazing impact on our lives. You can have living mentors whom you have never even met, yet they have influenced you through their books, tapes and seminars. You may have mentors who touch your life briefly, leaving after they've accomplished their mentoring roles.

Are mentors perfect? Or course not. They make mistakes, just like everyone else. The difference is they have learned from their mistakes, and they want to share that knowledge with you.

Where Can You Find A Mentor?

At every stage of your life, look around and find the person you want to be like. It should be someone you can relate to. It doesn't matter that you may not know them. Mentors are very open, and they are seeking to share their wisdom with others. A popular and famous quote goes something like this: "When the student is ready, the teacher will appear." Are you ready for your teacher?

The Business Mentor & the "Secret Ingredient"

After graduating from college, the young man started working with a large multi-national corporation. However, it had always been his dream to start his own business, but he didn't know how to go about it. So, he started a business on a part-time basis.

His business mentor took him under his wings and began coaching him. He gave the young man his first lesson: "There are No Secrets". It's all about hard work. The harder you work, the luckier you are. However, by adding one secret ingredient to that hard work you will increase the likelihood of always reaching your goals.

"You can have anything you want", said his business mentor. The young man was skeptical. "Anything? How is that possible?" he asked. The mentor then handed him the secret ingredient that would make it possible, and explained how it works.

"It is called a 'collage', or a 'dream board'. All you have to do is simply get a piece of cardboard about 24 inches by 24 inches. You then collect pictures of everything you want in life and start pasting them on this board. *Everything*." This is an amazing exercise in possibility thinking and, boy, is it fun!

The young man found pictures of the things he wanted: a new car, a computer, and his dream home. He even pasted pictures of the places he wished to travel to and visit. Going one step further, he found a toy replica of the car in the picture!

Everyday, he looked at his dream board and the replica car before he started working and came back to look at it whenever he could. It fired him up, and it inspired him. His dream board reminded him why he was in business. In a short time, he had fulfilled ALL of the goals and objectives on his 'collage', and more.

In his book "Think & Grow Rich", Napoleon Hill states, "Whatever your mind can conceive and believe, it can achieve". The young man found this to be very true as he continued to grow throughout his life. He found balance in his life with family, faith, friends and finances. The mind is a very powerful thing. Do not underestimate your capabilities.

In every stage of your life, you will continue to seek and find mentors. Your growth will accelerate as you learn to embrace the mentoring system of personal development. The experience of mentoring and being mentored will take you on a fascinating journey through life.

Can You Be a Mentor?

Being a mentor isn't all a matter of skills and abilities. It is more a matter of believing. It is a life philosophy. You have to love and want to help people. You have to "be there" for the people you are mentoring. Some of the best mentors are found in literary works. Books are an incredible source of knowledge, passion, and inspiration. Build yourself a big library and continue to add to it. Consider the following books, which have influenced many of us:

"How to Win Friends and Influence People" by Dale Carnegie

"Think & Grow Rich" by Napoleon Hill (www.nightingale.com)

"The 7 Habits of Highly Effective People" by Stephen Covey (www.stephencovey.com)
"Seasons of Life" by Jim Rohn (www.jimrohn.com)

"The Road Less Traveled" by M. Scott Peck (www.mscottpeck.com)

"The Magic of Thinking Big" by David J. Schwartz
"Chicken Soup for the Soul" series of books by Mark Victor Hansen and Jack Canfield. (www.chickensoup.com)

Whether you are mentoring a young child or a successful executive, "You've Gotta Believe" (YGB) you can help. There are some unshakable 'YGB's you should instill in the people you are mentoring:

YGB...
You Can Do It.

YGB...
You Will Get Better.

YGB...
There is a Great Future Ahead.

YGB...
Hard Work is Going to Make You Stronger.

YGB...
You Will Find the Answers to Your Problems.

YGB...
Your Dreams Will Come True.

YGB...
You Are Great!!!

And…. YOU'VE GOTTA BELIEVE that
YOU'VE GOTTA BELIEVE!!!

There is a quote that says, "To the world, you may not be someone; but to someONE, you may be the world".

To whom are YOU the world? Are you mentoring someone? Are you helping someone say yes to their dreams?

Always Remember:
You GOTTA Believe!

- Hasnain Khaku -

Brian Tracy

The following article was submitted by Brian Tracy, the most listened to audio author on personal and business success in the world today. He is the author/narrator of countless best-selling audio learning programs and the author of 16 books. All rights reserved worldwide. Copyright © 2006.

Contact Brian Tracy at:
Brian Tracy International
462 Stevens Ave., Suite 202
Solana Beach, CA 92075
Phone: (858) 481-2977
www.BrianTracy.com

Chapter 6

How to Write a Book

Brian Tracy

Introduction by Don Boyer:

The power of the written word is astonishing. Every time you open a book, you are inviting new thoughts, ideas, suggestions, and perceptions into your life. Books are the keys that unlock the doors to success. Whether they are penned for entertainment, education, or personal and professional growth, they are an invaluable tool for enriching millions of lives. A single book can be the sole driving force of inspiration and motivation to unleash your hidden talents and fulfill your dreams. Imagine that!

With that thought in mind, I'd like to introduce you to Brian Tracy, a remarkably successful author and international speaker. Brian is a renowned authority on personal, financial, sales, and business success.

A passionate reader, Brian also believes that books have the power to change lives.

He has written numerous audio-learning programs and 16 books with that purpose in mind. Read on as Brian takes us through each step and shares first-hand knowledge of the art of writing a book.

Don Boyer

How to Write a Book

Brian Tracy

1. Start with a message, idea, story that you really want to share with other people.

2. You must be an expert on your subject. You must know 10 words for every word you write. If you write on success, you must already be successful. If you write on money, you must already be rich. If you write on relationships, you must already be happily married.

3. Define your target market, exactly *who* are you writing this book for?

4. Make sure that your market is large enough, containing 100,000 to 1,000,000 potential book buyers.

5. Buy, read, find out everything you can about other authors, books, or articles dealing with the same subject. Make sure your material is different and better in at least *three* ways.

6. Gather all the information that you will need to write your book. Do your research and homework before you start to write.

7. Organize your material into seven, ten, twelve, or twenty-one chapters, each following in a logical order, from beginning to end.

8. Write out every key point in each chapter on a legal-sized writing pad.

9. Organize your points from #1 through to the closing part of the chapter. Do this for every chapter until you have a separate "down dump" of all the key ideas.

10. Begin with Chapter One and dictate the book in the order of material you have chosen

11. Once you have dictated the entire book, have a typist type it out and give it back to you by email or disc for your computer.

12. Set up a work schedule with blocks of time of two, three, or four hours. Discipline yourself to sit at the keyboard and edit during this time.

13. Edit the entire book from front to back the first time. Correct the grammar and typing errors. Create the necessary paragraphs. This is the longest, hardest job of editing in the whole book.

14. Write an Introduction, a Preface and Acknowledgements, if necessary.

15. In your *second* edit, break up the text with a heading every two, three, four paragraphs. Make it "bite-sized" and easy to read.

16. In your *third* edit, place a quote at the beginning of each chapter. Create three, five or seven action steps at the end of each chapter if it is a self-help or educational book.

17. In your *fourth* edit, which will take much less time, polish the sentences, delete unnecessary material, make final corrections.

18. In your *fifth* edit, completely reread the entire book from cover to cover. This takes the least amount of time of all.

19. The entire process above requires 50 – 100 hours of work, once you have gathered all your material.

20. Always play gentle classical music in the background. Best of all, get headphones and listen to classical music while you work. Music makes you more alert, creative and fluent.

Brian Tracy's 3 personal success mottos:
Just Do It!
Make It Happen!
Never Give Up!

- Brian Tracy -

Jerry Haines

Jerry Haines has devoted his life to the study of the fundamentals of human behavior. Based on his 30 year association with Jim Rohn, he has made a career of understanding personal motivation and how it affects performance. Jerry is recognized as a talented speaker and effective trainer. He has spoken to over 11,000 companies covering topics like: Winning Through the Refinement of Philosophy, The Importance of Discipline in Our Life, The Five Most Important Lessons to Learn and Developing a Game Plan for Living Your Life on Purpose. You can contact Jerry at 800-553-0840 or email glhent@earthlink.net, or you can visit his website: strivingforgreatness.com.

Chapter 7

Welcome The Disciplines That Can Change Your Life

Jerry Haines

Discipline. That ugly word. What do you think of when you hear the word *discipline?* Some people have told me they think of whips and chains. Others say we need some of that around here, whether it's in their office or at home. Still others have bad memories of being disciplined in their youth. I was raised in a very strict family. My Dad, God rest his soul, was tough on me. He wanted to make sure I had good work habits, good school homework habits, good manners, and good morals and values. As I said, he was tough. Then in 1975, I find myself in a seminar listening to the great business philosopher Jim Rohn talk about discipline and how to embrace daily disciplines in order to have a good life. He said, "Discipline is that bridge we all must cross from being inspired and having dreams and turning all that into reality."

After I heard that statement, I said to myself, "Now I get it. Self-discipline is a good thing." With a new attitude, I decided to welcome the disciplines that could change my life. I looked at the benefits of discipline and realized how my direction and life would change greatly if I were more disciplined. First of all, true discipline is not easy. However, the rewards of being a self-disciplined person encouraged me to welcome any discipline that could change my life for the better. Some of the reasons why you should choose a self-disciplined lifestyle, rather than one of ease, are listed below.

- Disciplined activity can discover untold miracles, uncover unique possibilities, opportunities and strive to fulfill your natural potential.

- Discipline enables you to capture your emotions and the wisdom needed to translate them into action.

- Self-discipline affects how you see yourself. Your self-image is so much better when you know you can do whatever it takes to succeed and change. Lack of discipline is a source of low self-esteem. As Jim Rohn says, "Lack of self-confidence comes from not what you can't do, rather it comes from what you can do and don't do."

Here are some disciplines to welcome that can make major changes in your life:

First, we use discipline to control our thoughts. Confused thoughts lead to confused results. Mental exercises will produce good thinking habits which enable us to make better choices, resulting in a more fruitful life.

Secondly, discipline yourself to get in the habit of sending a greeting card every day to someone you care about. I got in the habit of doing that about six months ago, and it has added much value to my life. The person receiving my card feels appreciated, and I feel good that I made the effort to affect someone's life in a positive way with my heartfelt message.

Thirdly, when you are disciplined to enhance your health, you will curb sickness.

Fourth, discipline your use of time. Time is a constant, so we must improve how we manage it. Becoming disciplined in this area will enable us to accomplish so much more in our lives. The best way for me to get more value out of my time is to develop a detailed plan of action for every important part of my life.

Fifth, discipline yourself so that you take nothing for granted, because the things you take for granted usually disappear. Everything of value in your life requires constant care and attention.

There are so many positive aspects to being a truly self-disciplined person. By engaging in the daily disciplines, I am better able to stay on track and focused. The best way to stay on track and focused is to paint a clear picture and view of your future on paper. Having a detailed plan of action creates excitement because you can clearly see the promise of what is to come. Remember: The promise of the future is an awesome force if it is well designed. It is much easier to pay the price if we can see the promise of the future very clearly. I don't mind paying the price when I exercise at my home gym four or five times per week, because I know that I will benefit by feeling better, both mentally and physically. I don't mind making my daily phone calls to follow up or generate new business because I know that effort will provide me with a good financial future. I welcome the disciplines that enhance my relationship with my wife, that keep me in control of my health, time, work habits, communication, sleep, etc.

The rewards of a disciplined life are abundant, although they may not be received until much later in life. Beware of and avoid delaying or putting off what needs to be done today. Most people, and I have been guilty of this, would rather choose today's pleasure over tomorrow's fortune and rewards. Instead of doing it now, most people think about doing it later; that's called procrastination.

The best way to get in the habit of being a truly disciplined person is to start with a new discipline. For example, let's say you begin exercising 30 minutes 3 to 4 times a week. After a while, you begin to notice the results. The excitement you get from seeing those results will entice you to eagerly maintain your new discipline and help you develop a habit which can lead to other disciplines, such as eating healthier.

Remember, it takes consistent discipline and consistent effort to master the art of setting goals, time management, leadership, parenting and relationships, etc. It also takes persistence to maintain the activity when you do not feel motivated. My experience has shown that, if I keep at it, I'll eventually get the results I'm looking for. Those results motivate me, leading me to press on toward other disciplines with a more enthusiastic attitude. Also, the reason I keep pressing on is because, as you probably know, all good things in life are upstream. Finally, as my good friend Ron Reynolds says, "Discipline is like a set of magic keys that can unlock all the doors of wealth and happiness." That is a terrific reason to welcome the disciplines that can change your life.

Live your life on purpose,
and with a purpose.

- Jerry Haines -

Glen Curry

Glen Curry is the founder of "Fine Tuned for Success." He is dedicated to help those who desire a higher level of success find the motivation and tools they need to win in life. A dynamic public speaker, radio personality and author, Glen has developed many tools for success. No winner should be without his cards, "Principles of Success for Champions and Winners." To view or order Glen's life changing materials and tools for victory, success and prosperity, please visit his website at www.finetunedforsuccess.com. Glen can be contacted at glencurry@finetunedforsuccess.com.

Chapter 8

Principles of the Wealthy

Glen Curry

I married into a great, but diverse, family. There are family members who are successful business people, while other members are on public assistance or welfare. Some are broke, and others are millionaires many times over. Some have Ph.D.'s, one is a nuclear physicist and others failed to graduate from high school.

When I got married, my mother and father-in-law lived in a 7,000 square foot, three-story custom built house in Southern California and drove a Rolls Royce. (Actually they've had three Rolls Royce's since I've known them.) In addition to this, they also owned several additional homes that they lived in at the same time.

This is an extreme contrast to other family members who were and still are unemployed, down and out, and having to freeload off their parents, the government, or anyone else who will give them a handout.

I'm not saying they aren't all nice, sincere, loving people. I am saying some are successful, happy and rich; others struggle, are unhappy and poor.

Why the Huge Gap in Prosperity?

What I've come to discover is that there is a vast difference in how people think and what they believe. These factors are reflected in the prosperity, success, and happiness that people enjoy.

Simply put, rich people think differently than average people. Rich people talk differently than average people talk. Rich people believe differently than average people believe. Rich people listen to different things than average people do and listen to things differently than average people. Rich people also utilize their time differently than the vast majority of people.

As an example of the different mentalities of the wealthy and the mediocre, consider gas prices. Gasoline prices have risen to an incredible three plus dollars per gallon. The average person automatically blames the oil companies and the President for price gouging (I'm not saying they aren't correct) and then begins making plans to cut back, do without, and find a more economical vehicle or maybe even consider trading their car in for a bicycle.

The rich, on the other hand, may not like the high price of gas, but will never consider cutting back or doing without their gas-guzzling rides. They get busy and formulate a plan to create more wealth to cover the higher prices. Their mentality is totally different than the average person. You must start thinking like the rich to attract riches.

The Rich Think Differently Than the Mediocre!!!

The wealthy are usually 'possibility thinkers', while the mediocre tend to be 'impossibility thinkers' who always have a reason for why things can't be done. The average person makes excuses, while the rich makes things happen. Someone said, "Average is the worst of the best and the best of the worst."

As I observed our combined family, I discovered that some of the millionaires had no formal education to speak of, while some of the poorest members were the most educated, actually having college degrees.

That being true, I had to conclude that education does not guarantee prosperity and success; neither does a lack of formal education guarantee poverty. It's something else!

It's a Different Mentality and Different Habits!!!

When asked about his prospects for the future, one of the unemployed family members said it didn't look good. When asked why, he replied, "I don't have any money, and I can't get a job because I don't have a high school diploma." When it was suggested that he should get his GED (the equivalent of a high school diploma that you can receive in a very short time online) and then get a job, his comment was, "I'm too busy to get my GED." My thought was "too busy doing what? Certainly not making money or enjoying life or being a blessing to your family."

I asked this adult man (my nephew) what he did all day; and he replied, "I take naps and play video games."

In sharp contrast to that mentality, at a recent funeral, I spoke to one of my wife's cousins who is a multi-millionaire (most of you would know his name if I said it) in his late sixties or early seventies. He said he loved his life and would never retire. He went on to say he was busy all the time, had the energy of a forty-year old, and that his mind was full of beneficial money making ideas for businesses that he wants to try.

Fix a Race Car or Own a Race Car?

If a kid from the poor side of town, with poor parents, loves race cars, his goal in life might be to grow up and work with a pit crew or even someday gain enough knowledge to work on race car engines. His goal is to do anything to be close to the action he loves.

Now, compare that mentality with a kid that comes from an upscale neighborhood with successful, wealthy parents. This child might also love race cars like the child mentioned above. However, because of a different mentality, the well-to-do child doesn't think about working with the pit crew, he thinks about owning a race car and hiring a team of dedicated people (like the kid mentioned above) to be his pit crew and mechanics and make him a winner. His upbringing, surroundings, and the mentorship of successful parents enabled him to dream larger than the average or poor child.

It Doesn't Seem Fair, but That's the Way It Is!!!

Perhaps you weren't surrounded with success and great role models, coaches or mentors when you grew up, and you identify with the first child. The good news is you can change your thinking, talking, habits and belief system which will then cause you to attract success.

If the idea of you personally being happy, successful and prosperous is a new concept to you, get ready for a battle! It's a battle you can definitely win, but it's a battle nevertheless. I will attempt in this short chapter to give you observations and principles that will be helpful in turning your "lemon into lemonade"; but the bottom line is, it's up to you. A man once wisely rhymed, "If it is to be, it's up to me."

Did you know that generally speaking, success magazines such as "Forbes, Success, Entrepreneur, Inc." as well as all of the others aren't even available on the newsstands in lower income neighborhoods? Different information is available to wealthy people than average people. You are reading this book because you are hungry for uncommon information that will help you make wise decisions and win in life.

My attitude is; "Hey, if I'm scratching the ground with a stick trying to dig a hole, and you've discovered that there is such a thing as a shovel, I expect you to tell me." That's what mentors do; they show you a better way by giving you information to help you live your life more effectively.

The Successful Talk Differently than the Average!!!

I was standing in line at the U.S. Customs in Miami and overheard several people talking about the horrible mess someone who seemed very near and dear to them was in. On and on they went about this person's difficulty, and each offered their ideas about what this person should do to solve his problem.

It was none of my business, and I usually don't, but this time I couldn't help from eavesdropping because the events sounded so juicy. I was beginning to feel sorry for the person in their conversation when it occurred to me that these people weren't talking about a mutual friend or relative, they were talking about a soap opera character that they watch everyday on TV. I felt foolish, but I also learned something important. The average person lives their life vicariously through other people (thus the huge sales of the National Enquirer, People magazine, etc.), while successful people live their own lives on their own terms. They do in reality what others only read and daydream about.

Stop Daydreaming and Start Doing!!!

The successful people I've been exposed to don't talk much about TV shows. Actually, they prefer to read instead of watching TV. They talk about their magnificent obsessions, what they are currently doing, their future goals, and projects they are involved with.

The successful rarely complain and insist on talking about positive things instead of negative things. (You should copy that habit beginning right now!) They always ask questions that will further their education and cause. They take responsibility for what happens in their lives and hate excuses. You will never hear a successful person say, "That's not my job" or "thank God it's Friday." If you catch yourself saying either of those things, immediately take out a twenty dollar bill and burn it up to make an impression on yourself that your attitude is costing you money.

The average always speaks about the benefits of things they don't have, while failing to utilize what they do have. The rich do the opposite. They endeavor to utilize what they do have to the fullest, knowing that that is the way to materialize what they don't have.

The Successful Utilize Their Time Differently than the Average!!!

If you have the opportunity, go into a doctor's office waiting room in a poor neighborhood and just sit and observe what the people waiting to see the doctor are doing - then drive to an upscale neighborhood and do the same.

Nearly everyone in the poor neighborhood will be watching the waiting room TV. Nearly everyone in the waiting room in the wealthy neighborhood will be reading a book. The wealthy redeem their time by reading to further their education or read for pleasure. The poor accept and watch whatever someone else chooses to put on.

The Poor Waste Time. The Average Spend Time. The Rich Invest Time!!!

Every five years, you must renew your driver's license in California. In Los Angeles County, that means that most people will spend an unpleasant hour or two waiting in long lines with hundreds of frustrated strangers. These frustrated people will go through the same time-consuming, boring ritual every five years until they die.

What I've discovered is that the successful people avoid a lot of this misery by doing what the poor and mediocre could have done but didn't do. They call a few days ahead and make an appointment, thus enabling them to go directly to the front of the line.

The reason I'm giving you these comparisons and observations is so that you and I can learn and implement these success habits and principles in our own lives. Since we are dealing with fixed scientific laws, when we do what successful people do, we will get their results – success!

The Rich Make the Most of Every Moment!!!

I really like "oldies but goodies" music, especially while I am driving. I could listen and sing along to those songs for hours. Even though I really enjoy the hits of the 50's and 60's, they have never given me one red cent. Therefore, I invest my time listening to material that will bring wealth into my life. I make my drive time part of my "becoming fine tuned for success" time by listening to CD's of successful men and women sharing principles of success and leadership.

Millions of people wake up Monday thru Friday dreading their drive time. Why not wake up looking forward to drive time knowing that you are going to learn something wonderful and valuable as you drive? What you learn by listening to success motivation speakers may never get you a college degree, but it may bring you a greater degree of happiness, self-confidence and millions of dollars into your life.

You will find that successful people develop a plan for their day and stick to their plan. They use Day Timers, computers, Palm Pilots or other helpful systems to schedule their day, thus squeezing the most productivity out of their time.

The Rich Listen to Different Things than the Average!!!

Those who have resigned themselves to second-rate, so-so lives treat their own ears like garbage cans. They listen to fear, doubt, unbelief, can't make it, never get ahead, never had anything and never will information, songs and programs. They become experts on why something positive and rewarding can't be done. They have bought into the lie that they will never have it any better than they do right now; and, of course, it's someone else's fault.

The defeated in life resist hearing anything that will raise their hopes. The rich only listen to things which will lift their hopes, and then they get busy gaining the knowledge to materialize those hopes.

Not only do the rich listen to different things than the average do, they also listen differently if they happen to hear the same thing. What I mean is that a successful person, through discipline, develops a sort of filtering system that doesn't allow him to accept lies, seeds of failure and lack, and other negative things he hears. The wealthy aren't as gullible when it comes to a negative report as the ordinary person. The successful know that "they" control their destiny, not some news report or some so-called expert.

The Successful Do Daily what the Average Person Only Does Occasionally!!

Successful people have the revelation that **"the secret of my future is hidden in my daily routine."** Memorize that statement and master its meaning! Discipline yourself to do things daily that move you closer to your dreams and desires. This revelation will enable you to act on opportunities that the average person wouldn't even recognize.

Those without a lot of money tend to believe that rich people are basically lucky and haven't experienced the setbacks that they have in life. In answer to that excuse, one rich man said, "That may be true, but along the way I discovered that the harder and more intelligently I worked, the luckier I became."

The Wealthy Know What to Ignore!!!

The throbbing pain of a minor burn or cut is a continual reminder that you are physically hurt. In like manner, strife, bitterness, unforgiveness, hurt feelings, jealously or anger become nagging reminders that you hurt emotionally. Successful people, no matter how rich, know that they can't afford the luxury of dragging those disempowering weights through life. Because an agitated mind kills creativity and productivity, successful people refuse to harbor such things. They have learned to simply "let it go". You must do the same!

You Will Make More Money in Your Lifetime if You Take Great Vacations – Frequently!

A peaceful mind thinks better, makes better decisions, and is more creative. No one can stay in the battle without a break without breaking. We need to get away, see and do things out of the ordinary and recharge our batteries.

Millions of hard-working Americans utilize their vacations to paint their houses, catch up on chores, or lay around the house. THAT'S NOT A VACATION! If you return to work unrefreshed, uninspired and in the same rut, you still need a vacation.

It sounds unscientific or even crazy, but I believe you will make more money in your lifetime if you take great vacations – frequently. Living in Southern California my eyes see mainly gray. I live in a stressful concrete jungle. The freeways, parking lots and streets are gray, the concrete buildings are gray, the trees are a greenish gray covered with grit and grime, even the smoggy sky and air we breathe is gray. God designed our eyes to see hundreds of shades of greens and blues.

I don't want to recommend that you go in debt to take a vacation, but in a sense, if you go somewhere that inspires you, rests and refreshes you, enlarges your vision and changes your life – it's worth it.

My wife and I were workaholics for years, never taking a day off for ourselves for any reason. We thought that the only principle to gaining wealth was hard work.

One year we went to Hawaii, and it changed our lives. We now go to Maui every March and August, Aruba in November, and Atlantis in the Bahamas every May. I can honestly tell you that we are happier, more creative, productive and accomplish much more than we ever did working seven days a week year after year.

Personally, I enjoy the islands, scuba diving, boating, seeing crystal clear water and breathing fresh air. That may not be what inspires and refreshes you. Go somewhere you've dreamed about and watch how it increases your capacity to believe for bigger things. Take a vacation that impresses you.

To Change Your World…

- Change your thinking, talking, and what you hear.

- Develop a "can do" belief system.

- Develop beneficial habits and drop the bad ones.

- Make the most of your time and schedule your day.

- Know what to ignore.

- Take great vacations.

You Can Do It!
You Can Win in Life!

- Glen Curry -

Melinda Boyer

Melinda Boyer is an up-and-coming speaker and writer. She is the co-founder of Real Life Teaching and Real Life Publishing along with her husband, Don Boyer. She is the mother of three wonderful children, Manuel, Marco, and Marina, and a beautiful new granddaughter "Mariah". You can contact Melinda Boyer at melindaboyer@realifeteaching.com.

Chapter 9

Steps To The Top
"Believe in Yourself"

Melinda Boyer

*We all experience times when we don't
know where we are going or
how we're going to get there.*

With that sentiment in mind, I'd like to share a little story with you. The year was 1993, and my father had gone back to school. At the time, I had no idea how much his accomplishment would impact my life. After my father completed his studies and graduated, I was influenced beyond measure. I was very proud of him for returning to school after a lapse of many years; and the fact that he did so when he was 50 years old absolutely amazed me. At first, I remember thinking "my dad is really smart". As the significance of his achievement sank in, I thought 'Wow! I'm so very impressed!' Where did he get the motivation and the drive to go back to school after so many years? The answer was quite simple – he believed in himself and knew he would succeed, regardless of the obstacles. He demonstrated that we are never too old to learn and to take new steps in order to accomplish anything our hearts desire.

At the time, I was working as a temp in the data entry department for a financial company. I knew if I was hired, the company would pay part of my schooling. That wasn't important to me at the time; I just wanted to get my foot in the door. A position finally opened in customer service, and I applied for it and was hired. Now, the customer service area only had six employees: two were file clerks, three were customer service operators who took credit orders, and one person made all the files. Well, as you can guess, I was the one person who made the files and assisted the two clerks in their filing. Well I must have walked in the door right because after six months, I was backing up the three customer service operators. Within a month, I was taking orders.

Now, remember my father was going to college at the same time I began working in my dream job for a financial company. You see, for years I had wanted to be a suit person. What the heck is a suit person? Well, my image of a suit person was being important enough to wear a ladies suit to work and to carry a briefcase. You know like the prestigious business people they show on TV. I had finally made it - I was now a suit person. I had the suit and the job, but not the money, if you know what I mean.

The company I worked for was housed on 3 floors of a 16-story building. The 9th floor contained data entry, customer service, collections, credit analyst, file rooms and the mail room. One story up, on the 10th floor, were offices for account executives, secretaries, and auditors, as well as a reception area and a big conference room. A completely different division of the company was on the 11th floor. My goal was to climb my way out of the 9th floor and move on up to 10th. I promised myself that I was going to get there, but I didn't know how.

Then one day, I was asked to cover the Reception Desk on the 10th floor. I started talking to the executives, making sure I listened, asked questions, and paid close attention to them. Their actions and demeanor were very different than what I was used to, causing me to reflect on myself. I believed I was capable of moving up, but did I want to become an auditor or an executive? I finally decided to be an auditor, because they had the opportunity to leave the office and learn more about other companies. In order to reach my goal, I went back to school and took courses that would help me move up.

I had a direction, but how was I going to get there? The following five traits helped me step up to the top, and they can help you, too.

1. Believe in Yourself
2. A Desire to Succeed
3. Courage to Take the Necessary Steps
4. Focus
5. Ability to Visualize Yourself Already There

Ones I started applying these concepts, things began to change in my life. A position became available for a verifications clerk on the 10th floor, and as luck would have it, it was with the auditors! I applied and was chosen for the job. Within just months, I was managing the verifications department, which enabled me to accompany and assist the auditors on the audits.

Once you believe in yourself, you will be able to visualize yourself at the top. Nothing is ever out of your reach if you take the steps to move toward it. Too many people become so comfortable in their jobs that they become dormant. They wait for opportunities and success to come to them. The reality is that success is not going to just fall in your lap - you have to get up and reach for it. Focus on where you are going, close your eyes and see yourself there, then start to move toward it. Don't worry about what other people might say. They aren't living your life - you are. Right? So often, people listen to what others have to say instead of finding their own direction. When you follow your own direction and path in life, you work at your highest potential, and success comes much easier. In other words, don't follow someone else's blueprints; start drawing your own.

About five years ago. I found myself at the lowest point possible with no job and living with my parents again. I felt as if someone had taken the air out of my sail; I had no direction and was headed nowhere. Then it dawned on me that I had succeeded before, and I could do it again.

During this time, I did some heavy soul searching and had to learn how to believe in myself all over again. I realized I had to redevelop and apply the five traits in order to feel confident that I could take the steps to move up again.

Today, I have a wonderful husband who believes in me. It is so important in life to have a partner that truly believes in you and the things you do - it's like a double B12 shot of energy and excitement! It has provided such a boost in my life to know that someone truly believes in me as we work at our fullest potential together.

I am very thankful for the people that have been a part of my life, and I am very fortunate for the jobs I have held. I never thought for a minute that I was not capable of those jobs or achievements.

I would like to thank my Mom and Dad for always telling me that I was capable of anything I wanted to do and encouraging me to believe in myself. Through his example, my father was my first mentor. He taught me that it is never to late to pursue any dream or accomplish any goal. All I have to do is keep my head up and move forward, without looking back. Thanks, Dad.

Will you dream of achievement
or achieve your dream?

- Melinda Boyer -

Mel Brodsky

Mel Brodsky is a talented and much in demand speaker, corporate trainer and personal coach. He is the author of the highly acclaimed book, "Questions are the Answers". Mel can be contacted by phone at 888-909-8331 or e-mail at mel@youvegotmel.com or visit his website at www.youvegotmel.com.

Chapter 10

"It's Never Too Late To Make Your Life Great!"

Mel Brodsky

A grandson of slaves, George Dawson was born into poverty in 1898 in Marshall, Texas. Despite their hardships, George's father believed in the richness of life and raised his children to believe the same. Young George remembers when there were schools just for colored children, thus denying them of a quality, or even adequate education.

Since the age of four, he was always working to make money and help the family. At eight years old, he got a job feeding hogs in East Texas to bring extra money into the house. When George was twelve, he was rented out for $1.50 a month to work for a white family, the start of a long and hard-working life that left no time for a formal education.

But although George Dawson grew up in poverty, he was never poor. On the contrary, he was rich! Rich in attitude and in enthusiasm, and he had a zest for life unequaled by most. Through all his gargantuan challenges, Mister Dawson never whined, complained or indulged in self pity. He just did the best he could with what God gave him, living the life's lessons that his Mom and Dad instilled in him, that being, "work hard and respect other people".

Although George was considered illiterate, he never felt unintelligent; but he could recall how much he lost by not being able to read or write. There was the time he was working at a dairy farm and was up for a promotion and a raise; but when his boss asked him to sign his name on a contract, all he could do was mark an X, therefore negating the advancement.

One day at the ripe young age of 98, retired and tired of fishing, fate and destiny stepped in; and George Dawson became hooked on learning and was born again…. A recruiter for a literacy program in Dallas knocked on his door and invited him to take part in the community's educational program. "I've been alone for 10 years", Dawson told him. "It's time to put down my fishing rod and learn to read and write", which he did.

In 1998, Richard Glaubman, a schoolteacher outside of Seattle, Washington, read a newspaper article about Dawson. He was so impressed he shared George's story with his fourth grade students, which stimulated lots of curiosity and questions. As a result, Glaubman called Dawson and scheduled a visit. The visit evolved into a friendship and kinship resulting in the collaboration of the biography, "Life is So Good".

The George Dawson story opens with his vivid memory of witnessing a lynching in 1908 at the sensitive age of ten. However, Mister Dawson said he has no bitterness or regrets, just gratitude and thanksgiving for all that has blessed him, including sending all seven of his children to college. He just wished his beloved Mother could see him now and witness what she raised and what he has become. Dawson had gone from poverty and humble beginnings to being picked up in a chauffeur-driven limousine which escorted him to the Oprah Winfrey show, where he was her honored guest. That's got to be the WOW of all-time WOWS!!!

I met Mister Dawson for the first time while in Sacramento, California. The year was 2001. While driving to an appointment something was compelling me to stop and buy a newspaper. This confused me as I had stopped reading newspapers years ago because they're so negative. Fortunately, I followed my premonition and picked up that day's edition of USA Today. After rummaging through it, I came across an article about this most fascinating and unusual man. I immediately became smitten with him and purchased the paper. I cut out his article and threw away the rest of the paper. After highlighting the key points, I preserved his article by having it laminated.

Because I'm a motivational speaker, I thought if I shared Mister Dawson's story with my audiences, perhaps they would be also be inspired. I was correct; it turned out that they were very moved and inspired.

Then, I got lucky. While lecturing in Longmont, Washington, I reached into my briefcase and whipped out the original George Dawson newspaper article and shared it with my audience - as I always did. About two minutes into my presentation, a woman in the front row started to wave her hand with enthusiasm and vigor. When I inquired as to her exuberance, she said Mister Dawson was scheduled to do a book signing that evening at the Elliot book store in downtown Seattle and asked if I would like to join her at the event. I was speechless and blown away by the timing and expressed a resounding Yes! For a long time, it had been my goal to one day meet this extraordinary human being.

So on a rainy, stormy inclement evening, I braved the weather to meet this man; and I was not disappointed. That truly was a "golden moment" in my life as I came face to face with "My Hero and Role Model". This gentle, soft spoken, proud and dignified man touched my heart and my life in a meaningful and profound way that fateful day, not so much by what he said, but by what he was and the values he stood for.

Although he was 102 years of age, I felt he was "Destiny's Child" and was placed in front of me not only to influence my life, but so I could influence others by sharing our story. By the way, although Mister D. was a man of very few words, he could say more in one sentence than most could say in three volumes. Standing in front of him, I felt I was in the presence of greatness.

After a brief dialogue, we hugged and embraced; and I invited him to be my special and honored guest at my upcoming seminar in Dallas. I would seat him front row center; and with his permission, I would share his incredible story with an audience of 2,000 people. In all likelihood, he would receive a standing ovation from the sell-out crowd.

He looked at me somewhat embarrassed and humbled by the invitation and didn't know what to say or how to respond. When I realized I had put him in an awkward position, I retreated and told him I would call him when I got to "Big D".

Eight months later, I arrived in Dallas. One of the first things I did was call Mister Dawson. His secretary answered, and I said, "This is Mel Brodsky calling, may I speak to Mister Dawson, please?" She said I could not. I was taken aback by that response and said, "huh?" Then politely, I said "why not?" She said because Mr. Dawson died six months ago. My mind and body went totally numb and brought me to my emotional knees. When I regained my composure, I spoke to his secretary with conviction and resolve, saying "No! Mister Dawson didn't die! Mr. Dawson will never die! His life and his legacy will live forever as long as I have anything to do about it".
.
And so this book gives me the opportunity to keep that commitment to my "special friend"…

In summation, George Dawson is the personification of fulfilling your destiny. If you continue to be true to your core values and blend it with faith, persistence and patience, your good will come to you, "in God's perfect timing"…

My question to you is: Do you know who you are and what your destiny is? You do have one, you know.

You'll just have to live life to find out what it is…

God Bless.

Sincerely and with Love,

Mel Brodsky

Note: Mel Brodsky recreated and redefined himself in his sixties and has lived and accomplished more in the last 5 years then he did in the first 60. It is nothing less than a "Miracle" that he has gone from an ordinary life to the extraordinary one he now lives. Let George and Mel serve as an example that "It's never too late, to make your life great"…

> "To live your life with meaning is the greatest gift you can bestow upon yourself."
>
> - Mel Brodsky -

It's Never Too Late – Mel Brodsky

"I'm looking for a mentor who can show me how to get rich without boring me with a lot of advice."

Vic Johnson

Vic Johnson (vic@asamanthinketh.net) is an accomplished author, speaker and founder of five of the hottest personal development sites on the Internet, including www.AsAManThinketh.net, where he has given away over 300,000 e-Book copies of James Allen's classic book.

Chapter 11

Can You Believe It?

Vic Johnson

"Belief is the basis of all action, and this being so, the belief that dominates the hearts or mind is shown in the life." James Allen (Above Life's Turmoil)

William James, the great psychologist and writer of the early twentieth century, said, "Belief at the beginning of a doubtful undertaking is the one thing that will guarantee the success of any venture." You will rarely attempt something you don't believe possible and you will NEVER give 100% of your ability to something you don't believe in.

One of the best known stories about the power of belief is about Roger Bannister, the first person to run a mile in under four minutes. Before his accomplishment it was generally believed that the human body was incapable of such a feat. Bannister, who was a medical student, held another belief, however. "Fueled by my faith in my training, I will overcome all obstacles. I am brave! I am not afraid to face anyone on the track. I believe this is not a dream. It is my reality."

As soon as he broke the barrier, belief about the feat changed and his record only lasted 46 days. Within two years, more than fifty people also ran a sub-four-minute mile. Thousands have done so since, and today it's not uncommon for it to be done by a talented high-schooler. What happened in 1954 that hadn't happened in the previous 6,000 years of humankind that now allowed Bannister to achieve this? Did the human body change so that this could be done? No. But the human belief system did!

Perhaps my most favorite story about belief has a twist to it. Cynthia Kersey wrote about George Dantzig in *Unstoppable*. As a college student, George studied very hard and always late into the night. So late that he overslept one morning, arriving 20 minutes late for class. He quickly copied the two math problems on the board, assuming they were the homework assignment. It took him several days to work through the two problems, but finally he had a breakthrough and dropped the homework on the professor's desk the next day.

Later, on a Sunday morning, George was awakened at 6 a.m. by his excited professor. Since George was late for class, he hadn't heard the professor announce that the two unsolvable equations on the board were mathematical mind teasers that even Einstein hadn't been able to answer. But George Dantzig, BELIEVING that he was working on just ordinary homework problems, had solved not one, but two problems that had stumped mathematicians for thousands of years.

How many great things could you achieve if you just "believed" they were as easy as they really are?

Some years ago, I was listening to a friend of mine speaking to a business audience; and she quoted a teaching by David Schwartz from *The Magic of Thinking Big* that rocked my life. She said, "The size of your success is determined by the size of your belief." Now that was the first personal development book I ever read, and I've read it at least 20 times since. And I'm sure that I had heard that concept many times before that night. But it so impacted me that I wrote it down and must have looked at it a hundred times or more in the thirty days after that.

I spent the next few months focused on strengthening my belief in myself and in what I wanted to do. I took to heart what Wayne Dyer wrote in *You'll See It When You Believe It*: "Work each day on your thoughts rather than concentrating on your behavior. It is your thinking that creates the feelings that you have and ultimately your actions as well." So I worked each day on my beliefs by constantly affirming myself using written and verbal affirmations. The years since have been an incredible rocket ride.

Lest you think it's that easy, you should know that I WORKED HARD on my "belief thinking." The work dominated my life at that time because I was determined to change my beliefs. It's a lot like physical exercise; the more you do the stronger you become. I love what Emmet Fox wrote: "If you will change your mind concerning anything and absolutely keep it changed, that thing must and will change, too. It is the keeping up of the change in thought that is difficult. It calls for vigilance and determination."

Quite frankly, that's where most people miss the boat. They either half-heartedly try to change their belief systems or they don't stick with it long enough. Wallace D. Wattles, wrote "There is no labor from which most people shrink as they do from that of sustained and consecutive thought; it is the hardest work in the world." And yet it is the "sustained and consecutive thought" that is the first and primary labor of achievement.

Nightingale-Conant says Napoleon Hill is considered to have influenced more people into success than any other person in history. His most quoted line from *Think and Grow Rich* describes the power of belief, "Whatever your mind can conceive and believe, it can achieve." Just believing that statement, truly believing it deep down inside, is a bold step toward living your dreams.

Lisa Jimenez, in her great book *Conquer Fear!* writes, "Change your beliefs and you change your behaviors. Change your behaviors and you change your results. Change your results and you change your life."

So, how do you change your belief system?

1. **Prepare to win**.
    Nothing will strengthen your belief system more than knowing you're prepared. His pre-race

training was the key to Bannister's belief that he could achieve his goal. Remember his words, "Fueled by my faith in my training, I will overcome all obstacles."

2. **Take control of your thoughts**.
   It's your choice what you think about. Think success and that's what you get. Think failure and that's what you attract. To help in controlling your thoughts, make it a habit to affirm yourself. I had a box of business cards with an old address that I was going to discard. Instead, I flipped them over to the blank side and wrote affirmations on them. I had two identical sets, one for my car and one for my office. Throughout the day, I would read my "flash cards" aloud. (If you're in your car, only read while you're stopped for a traffic light ☺).

3. **Re-evaluate your situation**.
   One of my mentors, Bob Proctor, teaches that "our belief system is based on our evaluation of something. Frequently when we re-evaluate a situation our belief about that situation will change." And when you re-evaluate, spend more time looking at the positive side of your circumstances.

   In *Why Some Positive Thinkers Get Positive Results*, Dr. Norman Vincent Peale quotes "one of the wisest utterances I have ever heard in my lifetime," "Never build a case against yourself."

4. **Don't worry about "how-to-do-it."**
   One of my early mistakes was trying to figure out how I was going to do something before I'd believe I could do it. Start by believing you can do something, and the "how-to" will follow. Dr. Schwartz, again in *The Magic of Thinking Big*, writes, "Belief, strong belief, triggers the mind to figuring ways and means and how-to….those who believe they can move mountains, do. Those who believe they can't, cannot. Belief triggers the power to do."

   Interestingly, Dr. Schwartz wrote in 1959, "Currently, there is some talk of building a tunnel under the English Channel to connect England with the Continent. Whether this tunnel is ever built depends on whether responsible people believe it can be built." Even though they had no idea of "how-to-do-it" at the time, enough "responsible people" maintained a belief in this project and we have the famous Chunnel today.

5. **Finally, you must act.**
   The New Testament writer said, "Faith without works is dead." Until you act you're not committed and belief is not cemented. As Goethe wrote, "Until one is committed, there is hesitancy, the chance to draw back, always ineffectiveness." And your action and commitment will be greatly rewarded, for as he goes on to say, "Concerning all acts of initiative (and creation), there is one elementary truth, the ignorance of which kills countless ideas and splendid plans: that the

moment one definitely commits oneself, then providence moves too. All sorts of things occur to help one that would never otherwise have occurred."

What great challenge lies in your path today? Do you sincerely want to overcome or accomplish it? If the answer is yes, then CAN YOU BELIEVE IT? Can you believe the magic is really in YOU!

Recently, I was dramatically impressed by a passage in *The Message of a Master* by John McDonald. To me it sums up the reason why most of us don't have the belief to succeed: "The cause of the confusion prevailing in your mind that weakens your thoughts is the false belief that there is a power or powers outside you greater than the power within you."

And that's worth thinking about.

Change Your Thoughts,
Change Your Life

- Vic Johnson -

Matthew Kolling

Early in his career, Matthew Kolling was fortunate to work closely with such great mentors as Tom Hopkins, Brian Tracy, Jim Rohn, and Mark Victor Hansen. For over a decade, he has personally conducted over 9,000 seminars, addressing virtually every major sales organization in the country. Passionate about inspiring people, his messages serve to improve their lives and businesses from the inside out. The exciting and valuable information Matthew shares not only aids in recruiting and building better organizations, but also helps us to understand and communicate better with every person in our lives. Contact Matthew Kolling at:
Phone 1-877-271-7463
Email insighttraining@msn.com

Chapter 12

Happiness Is a Choice

Matthew Kolling

As an adult, I look back on my life and the choices I have made, and I realize that my life is an accumulation of those choices and the resulting experiences. Some of the choices which I thought were "bad" at the time actually turned out to be quite positive. Alternately, some of the "good" choices didn't pan out as well as I thought they would. Every experience is a stepping stone along the path of my life. That path is being laid as I walk; it doesn't matter how long it is, what it looks like or where it ultimately ends. What does matter is that I am the bricklayer and the path is my unique design. Each stone in our life represents an experience, regardless if it is good or bad, or right or wrong. We are an accumulation of those experiences, with our own voice, opinions, and ideas. If we believe something to be true, then it will become a reality. There are no exceptions. We create our reality with our beliefs; they are the building blocks which we use to build our life.

Creating Reality
Life is a masterpiece in progress, and we are continually creating and playing with this unique work of art. Sometimes we like what we've built and play with it for years. Yet, there are times when we knock it down and start over. The exciting part is that every decision,

every choice, is of our own making. We make those decisions every day by choosing where we focus our attention. We choose whether or not we want to be happy. Do you notice the beauty around you? Did you capture the radiance and sincerity in the smile of the person who just walked by? Did you take a moment to marvel at the splendor of a flower that has just blossomed?

The world is merely the outer reflection of who we are on the inside. During every moment of the day we create experiences through our beliefs, perceptions, and choices. Those beliefs accumulate and become the structure of our life. Remember, if we believe it to be true, we will experience it. Again, there are no exceptions. Understanding this, let's examine our beliefs, because they automatically cause us to feel and think in certain ways. Those thoughts and emotions serve as guides, directing our mental focus. The object of that focus creates our experiences and, ultimately, our lives.

Personality Plays a Role
Created early in our lives, our personality is only one part of the person we have become. It is simply a group of habits that we have developed, strengthened, and chosen to reinforce. It is the eye through which our minds perceive and view our reality. Our personality is our automatic pilot. It is not who we are, but what we do. It is not our identity; it is our behavior. The conscious mind is like a giant camera, and our personality directs its view and focus. Our personality

allows our mind to travel in certain directions and blocks its awareness of others. It has formed predictable habits very early in life, and we often become blind to those habits.

Every one of our beliefs has a result, and the same beliefs habitually repeated will create a permanent effect. If we like the effect, we seldom examine the belief. However, when we experience discomfort, we attempt to find the reason by looking for consistencies in our behavior and experiences. Unfortunately, we don't always notice what we are creating; therefore, we continue to create the same frustrating experiences. Our path soon becomes a circle, repeating itself over the years. Eventually, we tire of the same view and decide to move on.

Choices Change Experiences
The exciting thing is that we can choose different beliefs at any time. There is no work involved, no studying - it is done in the mind; it is a choice which is available to us all of the time. It is simple, but often not easy, because we hold strongly to these beliefs and have built our lives around them. They have created a safe place of familiarity. Although we struggle with dis-ease and may be unhappy or unmotivated, we stay with the familiar because familiarity breeds comfort. The unfamiliar is an unknown we must embrace; the unknown is the key to creating different experiences. We have heard many times "If we always do what we've always done, we'll always get what we've always gotten." Therefore, our reality never changes. If we

would like to create a different life, the key is to notice and accept the beliefs on which we've built our life, and simply choose again. Remember, if we believe it is true, then it will become our experience. The four steps outlined below will help in that process.

I.   Noticing Our Beliefs:

The first step in changing our path is to pay attention to our habits and our automatic responses. By consciously increasing our awareness, we will change how we view and see things. When we notice our experiences and how we respond to them, we open ourselves up to more choices.

We're not trying to <u>eliminate</u> or alter our belief systems; we're simply trying to accept them. You see, we identify with our strongest beliefs, and they become our truths. Many of these truths are simply automatic responses; and, therefore, they are not questioned. Because we assume they are truth, that is the only way we perceive them.

When we view our beliefs as the only real truths, we cannot understand and accept differing beliefs. This generates tremendous conflict in our lives. We must notice our beliefs and truths without judging them. Then, we can become aware and realize when they are no longer useful and can adjust them accordingly.

II.   Identifying / Recognizing:

Step two is the identification and recognition of the creations, expressions, and the aspects of your belief systems. This is the most extensive and time-consuming step in the process. We see our beliefs as the truth; therefore, we do not question them. They become invisible assumptions which color and form our personal experiences. Many false beliefs are accepted without hesitation because we have not examined them.

If we view our world within one little box, we do not see all of the possibilities. Our belief systems are our own little boxes. By recognizing and identifying these beliefs, we can broaden our horizons and expand our senses. As a result, we don't inhibit our thoughts or feelings, we just become more aware of them and their function. Increasing our awareness and expanding our senses allows us to experience so much more than what is in our own little box. So, by exploring and recognizing our behaviors and the effects, responses, and reactions to our beliefs, we open ourselves up to unlimited possibilities and opportunities.

III. Addressing Our Beliefs:

Once we've noticed and identified our beliefs, we can address them. Addressing our beliefs releases the energy required to feed and maintain our current belief systems.

Our thought process is designed to interpret only what our emotions, feelings, actions and experiences are communicating to us. Frequently, we refuse to accept certain thoughts or ideas because they conflict with other usually accepted ideas and beliefs. To change our experiences, we must change our focus of attention. When we change our focus of attention, obviously we will create different experiences. When we shift our attention to a different expression of a belief, we spark the energy needed to stimulate even more change.

Remember, our beliefs are like furniture that can be rearranged, changed, removed, discarded or replaced. After delving into our beliefs, we've recognized that they exist. We have not changed, eliminated or denied them. In this step, we move through our beliefs, letting go of the energy required to hold onto them. As a result, we lessen our conflicts and clear our mind of confusion. As we do this, our focus of attention takes on a sense of direction, enabling us to create new values and experiences with ease.

Simply address your belief and trace it back until you discover its root. Then, you can choose to keep it and continue to have the same experiences, or you can choose a different belief and open yourself up to new experiences. Doing this allows your experiences to be ones of choice, not the result of habit.

IV. Accepting:
The final step is accepting our belief systems with an "it matters not" attitude. It matters not if it is good or bad, right or wrong, or how others may judge it. If we worry about those things, we cannot accept ourselves or others, which creates internal conflict. Beliefs are neutral. Accepting those beliefs is the key which provides us with freedom of choice. Acceptance is not

an elimination of any element of our reality. Acceptance is the lack of judgment in any area of that reality. A genuine expression of support, love and compassion recognizes that each individual purposely creates every moment of their reality. There are no accidents, as it is intentional. No element of anyone's reality needs to be fixed, for it is not broken. We do not have the ability to change another person's beliefs or to create someone else's reality. We should focus our attention on ourselves, because the only control we have is in our own choices.

Happiness is a Choice
Our reality is redefined when we identify our beliefs, recognize our judgments, and allow ourselves to accept them. Through these actions, we can alter our reality.

Trust yourself to know what is best for you, for you know yourself better than anyone else does. You do not need to sway other people and win their approval and acceptance. "It matters not" to you. Don't worry about your neighbor's garden, tend to your own. Notice your beautiful flowers, and allow them to grow. It matters not how and when they grow, or how fast. The important thing is they will grow – it is inherent in their being. The same holds true for you.

If you believe it,
it will be so.

- Matthew Kolling -

David Corbin

Creatively blending pragmatic business experience with fun and humor, David Corbin has advised Presidents of AT&T, Hallmark, Sprint, the Sec. of Veterans Affairs and others. Thousands of people from CEO's to front line workers and sole business owners have benefited from David's concepts through speeches, lectures and trainings - live and on video. Davis is the author of <u>Psyched On Service</u>, <u>Illuminate</u>, <u>Brandslaughter</u>. To contact David Corbin, visit his website at www.davidcorbin.com.

Chapter 13

BRANDSLAUGHTER™
4 Powerful Steps to Avoid Committing Brand Homicide

David Corbin

How many times have you written off a restaurant because the waiter was a jerk? Or hated a name because you knew someone else with that name who rubs you the wrong way? Like you, people can completely turn off in a matter of minutes. In our mile a minute society, making split decisions is a necessary means of survival; filtering the barrage of messages that we breath like air molecules.

That's why as a leader in business (or leader of your own business), you better be sure that every molecule, every detail of your brand is consistent and in alignment with your vision.

Does the music you play in your office evoke a sense of peace, or does it give people that nervous feeling they get while waiting in the dentist chair? Do your employees deliver service with sincere respect for your product, or do they act with as much indifference as they do when flicking a cigarette butt?

These pieces of information combine with numerous others to make up the whole of your brand. Your responsibility is to notice if the pieces are congruent.

Unfortunately, there is no liability insurance for your brand. No nice forgiving deductible. It's as though you crashed your car in Mexico and your insurance doesn't cover accidents south of the border. Your car is totaled, and it only took a couple of seconds to crash - two seconds and a measly rock that spun your tires out. If only you could go back in time and slow down. If only you noticed that stupid rock.

Sad to say, it only takes seconds to crash your brand. That's what I call BRANDSLAUGHTER™. That hard-earned reputation, the 'good will', the whole 'shootin match' is done, gone, kerplunk. You've killed your brand and deserve to be convicted of Brandslaughter in the first degree.

Each of us can be that rock or rut in the road that destroys the beautifully crafted brand. So, how are you driving your Brand? With care.... or by speeding past those pain in the arse details that need to be smoothed out, paved over into your highway of success. Here's a four step process to 'insure' the value of your Brand.

1. **KNOW IT!**

    Take inventory as to how you interact with the marketplace. Is it how your phone is answered?

Is it your signage? Could it be your promotional material? Or maybe the way you dress? These are all impression generators, and they come into play when they are at the intersection of you or your staff and the marketplace. We refer to them as TOUCHPOINTS.

2. **LIVE IT!**

   Find examples of these 'branding intersections' or TOUCHPOINTS where you are supporting the Brand; where it is congruent with the desired Brand. For example your Brand is, in part, that you are innovative and you have the latest digital communication equipment before you.

3. **FIX IT!**

   Find examples in your 'branding intersections' or TOUCHPOINTS where you are undermining the Brand by being incongruent. For example, your Brand is to be extremely Customer-Focused, and your phone rings 20 times before you pick it up. This is where the 'rubber meets the road' and where the big payback is. For when you consciously engage in reducing the Brandslaughter, you will make quantum leaps in your market acceptance.

4. **EXPAND IT!**

   Make darned sure that you and everyone in your scope of influence are obtusely aware of the brand at all times. Foster a culture of brand awareness, brand touchpoints and opportunities to KNOW, LIVE, FIX and EXPAND the value of your brand.

Like I said, your brand has no liability insurance. So you better build a classic; a thunderbird, a heavy-door-old-school Ford or a car with no bucket seats between you and your baby; your business, in all its vulnerable beauty! And as with a real baby, I don't mean your lover this time, no action is neutral. You either feed the baby or starve it, nurture it or let it die from lack of touch. I don't mean to sound morose, but truly, your brand is an extension of yourself and it will either live or die. Therefore, carry it like a fragile egg and make sure your babysitters know how to hold it as well; supporting the head attached to a still floppy neck.

The growth is your reward. The appetite and curiosity that leads to more growth comes when you craft your brand with the touch it needs. With your care it can take in new inspiration and new endeavors that lead on and on and on and on...

Begin with yourself. Are you congruent with your brand? Would a close friend describe you with words that exist in your vision statement: truthful, energetic, a classic, invigorating, adaptable, etc.? Or are you incongruent with your brand and opening yourself up to be accused, tried and convicted of Brandslaughter©?

One thing is clear, your Brand is in your hands and in the hands of anyone who represents you. So don't crash your brand in Mexico. Rather, drive it smoothly and confidently to the checkered flags indicating goal achievement, market success and immense personal satisfaction.

*Accentuate the Positive,
Illuminate the Negative*

- David Corbin -

Gregory Scott Reid

Gregory Scott Reid is a well-known speaker and two-time #1 best-selling author of, *The Millionaire Mentor* and *Wake Up: Live the Life You Love*. Sign up for his no-cost Millionaire Mentor Newsletter at www.AlwaysGood.com. You can contact Greg Reid via email to:

>GregReid@AlwaysGood.com
>or go to his website at:
>http://alwaysgood.com

Chapter 14

What Goes Around, Comes Around

*Gregory Scott Reid
a.k.a The Millionaire Mentor*

Smile at others; they'll smile back. Extend your arm to shake a hand; someone else will reach their arm out and meet you halfway. Help someone else realize their dreams; they'll help you reach yours. It's that easy! You get as much in this life as you are willing to give. What goes around, comes around.

Now, you don't have to be a millionaire in order to have enough to give, but giving is one sure way to increase your chances of becoming a millionaire. I've always said the true rich have a heart of gold – their whole life glistens. When you reach out and help someone else sparkle, you shine! That's what mentoring is all about.

You might be asking yourself how helping someone else achieve their dreams can possibly help you achieve yours. If so, then you probably believe this is a competitive world, and we're all vying for the same spot on the ladder of success. I'm here to tell you that there is room for everybody at the top of that ladder. Mentorship is simply the key that removes the competition!

The secret that most people miss is, to get what we want, we should reach out to others and help them get what THEY want first. Then by the laws of affluence, our desires will be fulfilled in return.

To truly appreciate how mentorship works, visualize a boomerang. A boomerang is simple in design, consisting of two wings joined in the middle. These two wings don't compete against each other; they work together. Each wing contributes lift that keeps the boomerang in flight. With only one wing, it would never soar and would surely fall.

The boomerang is also designed to fly gracefully and smoothly. When thrown properly, it will spin and propel itself to its ultimate destination. Then, its path will curve itself right back to the person who threw it. Actually, when you throw a boomerang, you are the target!

It is easy to apply this concept to mentorship. Just think of one wing as the mentor, and the other wing as the mentee. They each provide the boost or lift that keeps the other from falling. Each wing creates a balance that helps to avoid any turbulence in its flight. Successful mentoring is sincere; it is a smooth process that enables the goals and dreams of both wings to take flight and soar. No matter how far that boomerang flies and how many successes it propels along the way, the ultimate success is when it comes back to its target – the thrower.

There are some people who believe that "boomerang" means to backfire. That just isn't so! A boomerang is designed so that it gently flutters on its return path, with its rewards hovering and waiting to be caught by its original holder. Like mentorship, it is an amazing concept of balance that exhilarates both wings along its flight!

If you want to succeed, eliminate the competition. Help someone else sparkle, and you'll be rewarded with a heart of gold while you, too, radiate in their glow. Is there anything richer in life?

Reverse the theory and find someone you admire to be your mentor. Their glisten will shine and reflect on you!

You see, true success requires both giving and receiving. What goes around, comes around. Like the boomerang, everything you give will come right back at ya!

Keep smiling!

*The greatest success we'll ever know
is helping others succeed and grow.*

- Gregory Scott Reid -

Charlie "Tremendous" Jones

Charlie "T" Jones, CPAE, RFC "Tremendous" Publisher-Motivator-Humorist. Thousands of audiences around the world have experienced nonstop laughter as Mr. "T" shares his ideas about life's most challenging situations in business and at home. Two of his speeches, "The Price of Leadership" and "Where Does Leadership Begin?" have been enjoyed by millions. He is the author and editor of nine books, including *Life is Tremendous* with more than 2,000,000 copies in print in 12 languages. To contact Charlie, please visit his website at www.executivebooks.com or call 800-233-2665.

Chapter 15

Books Are My Favorite Mentors

Charlie "Tremendous" Jones

Everyone who knows me knows my mentors are books. As a salesman, it was books; as a manager, it was books; in my home, its books; with my friends' lives, it's books. Years ago, I had a habit of giving everybody a book with my card. I hoped they were read; but if not, they were there to be read.

In his book, *You and Your Network*, my friend Fred Smith tells how Maxey Jarmon mentored him. I must admit that I felt a little envy as I read of their relationship. But, when I thought of all my tremendous mentors in books, I think of myself as the most blessed man in the world.

I would like to share with you one of the greatest ideas you will ever hear. A few simple changes in your daily routine can improve the quality of your life. From now on when you read a book, make the author your mentor and always read with your pen in your hand. As you get used to reading with a pen in your hand, you begin to cultivate the habit of making notes of things you actually think in addition to what you thought you read. We must learn to read, but only to get our minds in motion and start our thought processes.

I practice this in church. When the pastor starts to preach, I take out my pen and start making notes of things I think. This excites the pastor because he thinks I'm writing out his sermon. Sometimes I think he should throw away his sermon and use my notes. As I leave church, I get a smile or laugh when I say, "Pastor, you were really good this morning. You interrupted my train of thought a half dozen times." Whether it is selling, preaching, or teaching, interrupting their train of thought to help them see what they know will always bring a smile or a laugh.

Fifty years ago, I attended a lecture. I don't remember much of what the speaker said, but he made me laugh for an hour at my problems, as I identified with many principles that convinced me that even though we had never met, we were very much alike. As he closed his talk, he said, *"You are the same today that you will be five years from now except for two things – the people you meet and the books you read."* If you hang around achievers, you will be a better achiever; hang around thinkers, and you will be a better thinker; hand around givers, and you will be a better giver; but hang around a bunch of thumb-sucking complaining boneheads, and you will be a better thumb-sucking complaining bonehead. The "people you meet" and people you surround yourself with are your best mentors and a key influence in your life. We need mentors and positive role models as much as we need positive goals.

The trouble with our role models and heroes is that we can't take them home. We have got to grow and experience the lessons of life *alone*. But don't mistake aloneness for loneliness. Some people think they're lonely because they're young, while some people think they're lonely because they're old. Some people think they're lonely because they're poor, and some people think they're lonely because they are rich. Some discover that everybody is lonely to some degree, and that's the way it's supposed to be. You discover out of loneliness comes aloneness when you decide to live and grow. You alone decide to live your life and do your growing. No woman grows for a man. No man grows for a woman. No parent grows for a child. *When you grow, you grow alone*. Growing brings growing pains, but laughs come, too, if humor is part of your growing.

I mentioned "thinking with and listening and speaking to the heart", and about seeing things in perspective and learning to laugh at our growing pains, using humor to break down barriers in our own heart and between other people. But you will never realize these points in your everyday experience without the stimulus of reading that broadens your perspective and pulls you out of the negative cycles that can develop in your own thinking.

Here are some examples of my mentors in books:

General Patton made his troops mad and glad. He made them think and laugh when he wasn't around. General Patton once said, "If we're all thinking alike, somebody isn't thinking." When you're thinking, you're constantly discovering new dimensions to everything; when you're the wisest, you know the least; and when you're aware of your ignorance, you're the wisest. How good it is to realize my ignorance. General Patton said not to be afraid of fear, "Fear is like taking a cold shower. When the water is ice cold, don't tip-toe in – leap in and spread the pain around. *Success isn't how high you reach, success is how high you bounce every day when you hit bottom.*" Patton almost always helped his listeners see with their hearts what he was saying.

Abraham Lincoln is one of my favorite mentors. His life has served as an inspiration to people from all walks of life. Many people will tell you that one of the secrets of excellence is education, yet Lincoln had little formal education. His family was so poor that for a period in Lincoln's childhood, they didn't have a door to their cabin. The year after his mother died, eight people lived in a small one-room log cabin. Many believe if you're raised in poverty or a broken home, you don't have much of a chance of growing beyond your past.

There's a lot of emphasis on self-esteem today, yet Lincoln had little reason to believe in himself. His mother died when he was a boy. He had little time with his hard-working father. His sister died when she was in her teens. The woman he married didn't make his life a bowl of cherries. There were very few people in Lincoln's life who were there to stand by him and offer him positive encouragement of what he could and should do.

So, how does a man who lacks most of the things that we say you should have to be a successful leader, become one of the most revered heroes of world history? Two of the many great assets of Lincoln were his ability to tell stories in order to illustrate a point and, while doing so, get people to laugh with him. Much of this was stored in his mind and heart through the book mentors he loved as a boy. Lincoln was a great thinker, because he learned to *read and laugh*.

I would be remiss if I talked about mentors and my philosophy, and I didn't mention my mentor, Oswald Chambers. Nearly every word I have spoken for 50 years has been flavored by this man. Yet, it's no small wonder that many have never heard his name, because Chambers died in 1917 at age 43. He never wrote a book. How can I have thirty of his books if he never wrote a book? He married the Prime Minister of England's secretary, and when he went to work with the YMCA in Egypt during World War I, she went with him and made shorthand notes of his talks. When he died in 1917, she lived on for years and wrote all the books from the notes she'd made.

Let me tell you why Chambers is my favorite mentor. He challenges my everyday thinking with a warmth that has grown out of the struggles of his own heart. He helps me see how wrong I am in a way that lets me laugh at myself. Chambers says, "You can determine how lazy you are *by how much inspiration and motivation you need to do something*. If you're for real, you do it whether you feel like it or not. The best way to avoid work is to talk about it."

Get people to think with you, and you'll get them thinking better. Get them laughing, but don't let them laugh *at you*. Some comedians get people to laugh at them. And sometimes being a clown is necessary to loosen things up. But good managers, teachers, and salespeople learn how to get people to laugh *at themselves*. You begin by seeing things in perspective and learning to laugh at your own situation.

I urge you to read and motivate others to read. Never read to be smart, read to be real; never read to memorize, read to realize. Never read in order to learn more, but read to re-evaluate what you already know. Never read a lot, but read just enough to keep hungry and curious, getting younger as you get older.

Success for me is one word – thankfulness, learning to be thankful. The first mark of greatness is the first sign of smallness is thanklessness. An attitude thankfulness; of gratitude flavors everything you do. Once in a while, some young tiger will say to me, "Did you feel this way years ago when you didn't have anything?" I used to go home and say, "Honey, look at me. 'Man of the Month'. Look at this, 'Man of the Year'." She would say, "Where's the cash?" I'd say, "Honey, if we don't start learning to be happy when we have nothing, we won't be happy when we have everything." Well, I don't know if I ever sold her, but I finally bought it myself. I'm not trying to sell you; I'm buying it myself and sharing it. The one great thought, more than any other, is to be more grateful and thankful.

When you are in the game and wrestling with problems and achieving goals, the natural tendency is to focus on you. But, if you don't balance this with a perspective that realizes where other people are relative to you, with their need and goals, and realize the simple joy of living and growing through the stages of life, then all your goals and involvement, whether they're successful or not, will only lead to bitterness. The heart of success is thankfulness. When your heart is in a thankless state, you can laugh, but not at yourself.

When my family sits down to eat, our giving thanks goes something like this, "Dear God, we thank you for our food; but if we had no food, we would want to thank you just the same. Because, God, we want you to know we're not thankful for just what you give us, we're thankful most of all for the privilege of just learning to be thankful."

Thank you for sharing my thoughts. I hope you were thinking with me and that someday we'll meet and you'll tell me I interrupted your train of thought several times. May my thoughts help you realize that there are no mentors like books.

Business is never good business
until it makes a friend.

- Charlie "Tremendous" Jones -

A Life Changing Procedure – Zig Ziglar

Zig Ziglar

A talented author and speaker, Zig Ziglar has traveled over five million miles across the world delivering powerful life improvement messages, cultivating the energy of change. Since 1970, an extensive array of Ziglar audio, video, books, and training manuals have been utilized by small businesses, Fortune 500 companies, U.S. Government agencies, churches, school districts, prisons, and non-profit associations, In addition, Mr. Ziglar has written 24 celebrated books on personal growth, leadership, sales, faith, family, and success. To learn more call (800) 527-0306 or visit his website at www.ziglartraining.com.

Chapter 16

A Life-Changing Procedure

Zig Ziglar

"You can have everything in life you want if you will just help enough other people get what they want." Zig Ziglar

That's the motto of my friend, Zig Ziglar. It's not just a saying for Zig; it is indeed a way of life. Truly an American success story, he has dedicated his career to helping audiences around the world realize true personal and professional success. You are about to read Zig's oath which reveals that commitment and a positive attitude are winning traits in achieving our goals. Make a personal pledge to repeat it everyday, and you, too, will soon be saying YES! to your dreams.   Don Boyer

My Personal Commitment
Zig Ziglar

I, _____, am serious about setting and reaching my goals in life, so on this _____ day of _____, 20__ I promise myself that I will take the first step toward setting those goals.

I am willing to exchange temporary pleasures in the pursuit of happiness and the striving for excellence in the pursuit of my goals. I am willing to discipline my physical and emotional appetites to reach the long-range goals of happiness and accomplishment. I recognize that to reach my goals I must grow personally and have the right mental attitude, so I promise to specifically increase my knowledge in my chosen field and regularly read positive growth books and magazines. I will also attend lectures and seminars, take courses in personal growth and development. I will utilize my time more effectively by enrolling in Automobile University and listening to motivational and educational recordings while driving or performing routine tasks at home or in the yard. I will keep a list of my activities including the completion dates for each project in my Goals Program. I further promise to list good ideas (mine and those of others) and to note thoughts, power-phrases, and quotations which have meaning to me.

_____

Date   Signature

A Life-Changing Procedure

The eyes are the windows of the soul. So, to the person you are capable of becoming, each evening, just before you go to bed, stand in front of a mirror alone and in the first-person, present-tense, look yourself in the eye and repeat with passion and enthusiasm paragraphs A, B, C, and D. Repeat this process every morning and every evening from this day forward. Within one week you will notice remarkable changes in your life. After thirty days, add the procedure at the bottom of this card.

A. "I, _____, am an honest, intelligent, organized, responsible, committed, teachable person who is sober, loyal, and clearly understands that regardless of who signs my paycheck, I am self-employed. I am an optimistic, punctual, enthusiastic, goal-setting, smart working, self-starter who is a disciplined, focused, dependable, persistent positive thinker with great self-control, and am an energetic and diligent team player and hard worker who appreciates the opportunity my company and the free enterprise system offer me. I am thrifty with my resources and apply common sense to my daily tasks. I take honest pride in my competence, appearance and manners, and am motivated to be and do my best so that my healthy self-image will remain on solid ground. These are the qualities which enable me to manage myself and help give me employment security in a no job-security world.

B. "I, _____, am a compassionate, respectful encourager who is a considerate, generous, gentle, patient, caring, sensitive, personable, attentive, fun-loving person. I am a supportive, giving, and forgiving, clean, kind, unselfish, affectionate, loving, family-oriented, human being; and I am a sincere and open-minded good listener and a good-finder who is trustworthy, these are the qualities which enable me to build good relationships with my associates, neighbor, mate and family.

C. "I _____, am a person of integrity, with the faith and wisdom to know what I should do and the courage and convictions to follow through. I have the vision to manage myself and to lead others. I am authoritative, confident, and humbly grateful for the opportunity life offers me. I am fair, flexible, resourceful, creative, knowledgeable, decisive and an extra-miler with a servant's attitude who communicates well with others. I am a consistent, pragmatic teacher with character and a finely-tuned sense of humor. I am an honorable person and am balanced in my personal, family and business life, and have a passion for being, doing and learning more today so I can be, do and have more tomorrow.

D. "These are the qualities of the winner I was born to be, and I am fully committed to developing these marvelous qualities with which I have been entrusted. Tonight I'm going to sleep wonderfully well. I will dream powerful, positive dreams, I will awaken energized and refreshed; tomorrow's going to be magnificent, and my future is unlimited. Recognizing, claiming and developing these qualities which I already have gives me a legitimate chance to be happier, healthier, more prosperous, more secure, have more friends, greater peace of mind, better family relationships and legitimate hope that the future will be even better."

Repeat the process the next morning and close by saying, "These are the qualities of the winner I was born to be, and I will develop and use these qualities to achieve my worthy objectives. Today is a brand new day and it's mine to use in a marvelously productive way."

After 30 days, add the next step:
Choose your strongest quality and the one you feel needs the most work. Example: Strongest -- honest. Needs most work – organized. On a separate 3x5, print "I _____, am a completely honest person, and every day I am getting better at being organized." Keep this 3x5 card handy and read it out loud at every opportunity for one week. Repeat this process with the second strongest quality and the second one which needs the most work. Do this until you've completed the entire list. Use this self-talk procedure as long as you want to get more of the things money will buy and all of the things money won't buy.

Note: Because of some painful experiences in the past (betrayal, abuse, etc.) there might be a word or two that brings back unpleasant memories (example: discipline). Eliminate the word or substitute another word.

(Zig Ziglar's oath is also reprinted as affirmation cards at the back of this book. Cut them out and keep them handy for your daily pledge.)

It is not what happens to you that determines how far you go in life; It is what you do with what happens to you.
- Zig Ziglar -

George Ramirez

George Ramirez is an outstanding public speaker and trainer, covering business across the nation and being well traveled worldwide. His experience, along with his wit and wisdom, makes him a favorite in every audience. George resides in Whittier, California, along with his beautiful wife and life partner, Olivia Ramirez. He can be contacted at george@gengold.net or by calling (866) 945-4730.

Chapter 17

If It Walks Like A Duck...

George Ramirez

Does it really matter who we associate with? How much influence do our peers really have over us? Will it make a difference if we have a strong personality and are decisive in our actions? Let's explore what others have said about who we associate with...

"If it walks like a duck and it acts like a duck…….."

My guess is that 95% of the people will finish the above sentence the same way: "It must be a duck!" So what is the big mystery? Well, many times we are the last ones to notice that we are the ducks (or whatever else we are hanging out with at that time). Think back to high school and college. There were jocks, geeks, nerds, airheads, dorks, and wannabees. The frat and sorority groups were always there, as well as groups that were "lost in space", druggies, gothics, and metal heads. Some groups were defined along racial or political lines...Black, Brown, Socialist or Revolutionary. Today, there's Liberal, Progressive, Conservative, Left or Right Wing, it goes on and on.

Don't think that just because you got older and entered the "real world" that the labeling has stopped. Absolutely not! How many times have you heard "it's not what you know, it's who you know"? Well, I'm here to tell you that you have to be around them in order to know them, and who you know can certainly make or break you and your success. Before you say, "Who does he think he is, telling me I need somebody?", let's take a minute to look at just a few people who understand the power of association.

Pick any gang member and note the similarities and differences between that person and other gang members. You will soon discover that the list of likenesses is much longer than the differences. For example, their similarities may include hair, tattoos, clothing, style of speech, hand gestures, cars, music, hang outs, etc. These things are part of their identification, and the relatedness and values they share. They have an entire pecking order with common goals and a social order that will leave you speechless! Even if you don't agree with the purpose or end result, it is built upon association.

On a personal note, I've had the benefit of being friends with a person who served many years in federal prison. Now, relax! It was a long time ago, and he is now married and a productive member of society. Through many shared dinners and conversations with him, I learned a few things about his experience. Survival in prison is wholly based on who you know and your word, with zero tolerance if you try and BS your way with either. The stakes are much higher than when you or I try and "Dazzle a client with brilliance or baffle them with rhetoric".

Rarely, if ever, will fudging on our word, taxes, calendars or relationships cost us our lives. However, in the prison environment, it will! As strange as it may seem, that level of honesty is learned only through association. This is true whether it is one gang member to another, father to son, employer to employee, or mentor to mentee.

Let's look at another group. I'll call them the Wall Street, attorney, banker, doctor, politician, 21st century executive look alike, achieve alike, act alike (with a few differences of course) group. This group may not be a gang, but they hang out and associate with each other. Can a young attorney fresh out of law school benefit by associating with a more experienced, successful one? How about a doctor? Banker? Investment advisor? Anyone else…?

I believe there is no argument that great men like Henry Ford, Napoleon Hill, General Patton, Lee Iacocca, Zig Ziglar and many others have understood and truly benefited from the power of association. It is because of people like them that new voices that have taken up the call. Voices like Gregory S. Reid, Mel Brodsky, Will Cason, Don Boyer, the group at "What the Bleep", the directors of "The Secret", and, if you pay attention…You!

How will this information help you, and what do you do next? I am a strong believer in practical, take home, use it tonight stuff. I have experienced what I am about to share. This is not just some psycho-dabble theory from some professor who has never done it.

M.L.M. Stop!!! That's right, it's Multi-Level Marketing, network marketing, relationship marketing, or whatever you call it. The bottom line is that it is selling something to someone you know. You can call it "sharing" if you like that term better than selling. Because MLM's offer a great product, they are usually a better value for the money. The seller is usually a friend or someone you know. When a sale is made, the salesperson makes money, and so does everyone above them! Honest! I've done it, three times! I even made some real money at it, just not consistently. First, I will share the benefits of MLM, then the down side.

I believe everyone should try an MLM at least once. Be selective and shop around. Make sure you choose a good one! Don't sign up right away; do your research and ask questions. Why join? Join for what it will do to you, but mostly for you. Hopefully, the leaders will encourage you to pursue a path of personal development. This is a great way to learn new business and presentation skills, along with a few other disciplines you will never be exposed to in college or corporate America. More importantly, they will introduce you to the concept of listening to excellent CD's and reading awesome books. This will force you to shut off the TV, which in and of itself is probably worth the monthly obligation for your product. With God smiling upon you, this experience may help you find your true mentor. They hang out there, too.

Together, you may discover the things you truly love. However, there is a downside to MLM's.

You will never spend more money, make more phone calls, attend more meetings nor become more frustrated than in the MLM industry. You run the risk of joining the NFL (no friends/family left). Caller ID was invented because of MLM's. Your "guests" won't answer your calls; they will join the witness protection program; they promise to, but won't show up for your meetings; they will have you pacing up and down in the parking lot like a groom wondering where his bride is; they cancel the service/order; they lie - you get the picture.

So, once you get over it, here is what you do. Just like in a chicken dinner, you eat the meat and spit out the bones. Take the new disciplines, books, CD's, one or two great people, a newfound desire, a clear dream and vision of what you love to do. Hook up with the Millionaire Mentor Group; buy the book "Overachievement" by John Eliot, PhD.

Stop trying to keep it simple or duplicable, become fabulous, eccentric, joyful, grateful, energized, healthy, and look for others like yourself. You will become a magnet! The universe will line up with the desires of your heart. Others that walk, talk and act like you will show up... And they won't be ducks!

When the student is ready, the teacher will appear.
- George Ramirez -

Andrew Chapman

Portions of this chapter have been excerpted from Andrew Chapman's coming book *The 53 Biggest Self-Publishing Pitfalls and How to Avoid Them*. With over 23 years of experience in nearly every aspect of publishing, Chapman has trained thousands of people in his seminars around the world since 1999. Through his company, Author Training & Development, he teaches aspiring and existing authors how to achieve their goals and success. For more information, visit www.achapman.com.

Chapter 18

"Get Published Now!
You Just Have to Know How"

Andrew Chapman

Have you ever thought about writing a book? If you're like the majority of the population (81% by some indications), then your answer is yes. However, like many others you may not think it's possible. Do you believe you're not a good enough writer? Are you afraid to take a chance and give it a try; or do you think you're not smart enough? Maybe you just don't know where to start and how to go about it. Well, I'm here to tell you it's not only possible — you can do it!

In many ways, we're living in an unprecedented era. At no other time in history, have authors enjoyed the ability to have their works published as they do today If you've ever wanted to get published, now is the time. Especially for those of you in business for yourselves, becoming a published author should be a goal high on your list — it greatly enhances your credibility and brand identity, becomes a prime marketing tool, and can significantly increase your income.

We are fortunate to live in a time when we can create professional publications with relative ease and make them available to the entire world. So, while getting published through a traditional royalty arrangement with a publishing company is still difficult, we have many other ways to get published that didn't exist just over a decade ago.

There are people, old and young, from all walks of life, who have valuable information and stories to share. Since you are reading this book, you are most likely one of them. One single author joining the right words together in a sentence can have a life-changing effect on thousands or even millions of people. Those few choice words can even save a person's life. However, none of that can happen if those words remain solely in the author's mind.

So, how do you start? What does it take to get published? Well, the first step is to look inward, into yourself, and determine your burning desire. Perhaps, it's to entertain or to express yourself through the artistry of the written word, in which case humor, fiction, or poetry would likely be your vehicle. If you have a mission or calling, or are looking to promote your own business, then the nonfiction realm will be your avenue Or, perhaps you want to leave a legacy or lesson for generations to come, which would be done through a memoir, autobiography, or historical account.

Once you've determined what type of writing and message you want to share, you need to look at your goals and capabilities. The definition of success comes in different forms for different people, whether it is money, fame, authority, credibility, impact, or something else. Your goals will help determine the best path to your success. Your path to success is also affected by your capabilities. All successful people, in any discipline, have at one point or another assessed their own strengths and weaknesses. Make a list of yours as they relate to your project's vision, your resources (time and money), who you know, and what you know.

Lastly, you'll need to decide who your target readership is and how your book can capture their attention. For example, if your book will promote your business, then your target audience will be clients and potential clients — and you may promote your book by conducting seminars. If you are writing for another purpose, ask yourself, "Who would be most interested in what I have to say? Who am I trying to speak to?" It's simply not enough to say everyone will be interested or everyone is your target audience; you must be as specific as possible or your efforts will be diluted, diffused, and difficult.

Armed with the project you have in mind, your goals, your self-assessment, and your target audience, it's time to build a team. A mentor is the first step in building that team. Your mentor may be a publishing expert you happen to know, or if you don't know one, a professional who can act in this capacity. Typically, this professional is known as a publishing consultant, a book coach, or a book shepherd. This mentor's role is to help you create the path to success, based on your unique situation, and help build the team to make this possible. (You can certainly approach a book coach before you've assessed anything related to your project, but doing so will increase the cost of the coaching.)

Your team is built to fulfill the duties you are either unable or unwilling to fulfill; these are typically roles which reflect your weak points. For example, if you aren't a good writer, you will need a developmental editor. This is someone who can take your horrible writing and makes you look like a Pulitzer-prize winning author! If you don't have time to write, or are physically incapable, a "ghostwriter" can be hired to do the writing for you. In other words, there are no obstacles! Regardless of your circumstances, you can become a published author.

Aside from your team, your publishing mentor will also help you with the project itself — determining the best method and format for your situation. The methods are self-publishing, traditional publishing, or some hybrid of the two. The format is the physical form of your writing — book, booklet, card deck, calendar, electronic book or booklet, video, audio book, and so on. There are dozens of possibilities. I've used the word "book" to illustrate my point only because that's what people think of first when it comes to being a published author. However, your situation may be better suited for another format. Ideally, your mentor will help you to become published in multiple formats.

Finally, there's the marketing plan. Nothing happens without marketing. Your publishing mentor will work with you to develop your marketing strategy. The promotion of your project may be your responsibility or that of a team member. A very common misconception is that this is the duty of the publisher. That is not true. The publisher can be better described as promotional support — supporting you in your efforts to varying degrees. Thus, developing a clear and comprehensive marketing plan is critical to your project's success.

I can't emphasize enough that getting published isn't exclusive to the rich, the famous, the brilliant, or the lucky. All you need are your ideas, focus, and determination. While there are other paths to becoming a published author, I've shared with you what I believe to be the simplest (although not simple) and quickest path. A mentor magnifies your efforts.

It's my hope that this chapter and this book will help give *your* book, or other publishing project, every opportunity for success, regardless of you definition of success. As I mentioned, a single idea or thought can bring joy, meaning, clarity, understanding, or hope to someone right when they need it most. More than any other time in history, you have the ability to share your unique ideas, experience, and wisdom with the world through the power of publishing. Share it with us!

Self-publishing opens doors.
- Andrew Chapman -

Don Boyer
a.k.a "The Professor"

Don Boyer is a prolific writer, as well as an in-demand and sought after public speaker. He is the author of three mega-hit books: "Legends of Tithers and Givers", "The Power of Mentorship", and "The Power of Mentorship for the 21st Century", published by Real Life Publishing, and available on Amazon.com. He is also well known as the "Molecular Mentor" because of the "Professor Character" he created and plays while teaching the Science behind Success. To contact Don Boyer or to receive a free "Professor" CD, send an e-mail to donboyer@realifeteaching.com.

Chapter 19

The Science of Success

Don Boyer a.k.a. "The Professor"

Why am I known as the "Professor"? It is because I base my philosophy of success on quantum physics and immutable laws. Also, I created and portray a character known as the "The Professor". In this role, I become a mixture of Einstein and a professor dressed in a bright green suit, a loud purple tie, matching purple socks with a bright aqua blue shirt. Man, you really have got to see it to believe it! He looks like the nutty professor and dresses like a straight Liberace! Anyway, this wacky and colorful character teaches about success and achievement based on the laws of science - not on luck or chance. He also believes that the Bible is the most advanced scientific book that ever has been or ever will be written. The Professor says, "science does not prove the Bible, the Bible proves science", and I must agree.

If success was based on anything other than laws and principles, achievement in any area would be nothing more than a roll of the dice and a flip of the cards (which, by the way, is how most people interpret their life and the circumstances they experience). If life was really based on chance or luck, life on earth could not exist. Can you imagine if the sun's rising or the moon staying in place was a matter of chance or luck? If that was the case, there would be no such thing as life on earth. Our world is not based or formatted on chaos, but on order. It is based on structure and unchanging laws, and that is why we have life here on our planet.

Before you stick your finger in your ear, wiggle it up and down, and say 'Huh?'.... let me explain what all this science stuff has to do with reaching goals and creating wealth. Once you realize that achieving any goal or target you've set for yourself (regardless if it's financial or relational) is based on set laws that never fail, all you need to do is implement those laws. For instance, if you had a book in your hand and your goal was to have it hit the floor, what would you need to do? Just let go of the book, and the law of gravity will cause you to reach your goal. Pretty simple math, don't you agree? It's as simple as the following two laws. You can achieve your goals of success simply by implementing them.

You Can't Afford the Luxury of Negative Thinking

Do you realize that your thoughts can make you money or cost you money? Yep, that noodle sitting on top of your shoulders is an amazing thing. It will serve to bring you all the wealth you ever wanted, or rob you like a bandit until you are so poor you can't even pay attention. Okay, we need to get a little scientific here, so rub your eyes, shake your bootie or do whatever else you need to do in order to be alert. I think there was a song in the 70's called "Shake your Bootie, yea, Shake your Bootie". I said that to make you laugh and loosen you up! Okay, are you ready? Now let's get down to the science of our thoughts.

Everything in life is energy, which causes all forms of matter to be in constant motion. Good things are based on positive energy; bad things are based on negative energy. When you "Think" of good things, such as the desires of your heart, positive energy is released. Positive energy then attracts the good things you want, much like a magnet because they are of the same positive substance. Let's say you want to make $10,000 a month in cash flow. You begin thinking and visualizing about that $10,000.00 income. You envision all the things you will do and accomplish with that money. Positive energy is being released, and it is attracting that money to you. As those two positive forms of energy are moving towards each other, you start looking at your bills and thinking about debts. Then, instead of thinking positive thoughts, you begin to worry and are now thinking negative thoughts. Well, you've just broke the connection to "Houston".

That $10,000 a month in income stops flowing toward you because it no longer has a match or connection to you in the form of your positive thoughts. Oh, the law is still working because now you are sending out negative thoughts of lack and shortage. Those negative thoughts are out there attracting junk to you like a magnet. Those same negative thoughts are the reason everything is in shambles and your day has been a disaster, and then you hop into your car to go home, and the darn tire falls off! That is precisely why I say you *cannot* afford the luxury of negative thinking - it costs too darn much!

This is where many success gurus drop you off - they tell you what your problem is without giving you the solution to fix it. Hey, if I am broken down in the middle of the desert, I don't need someone pulling up, rolling down their window and saying, "Mister, your car is broken", then speeding off and leaving me stranded there. Throw me a cotton-pickin' bone, won't you? So, how do you keep positive thoughts about financial gain, when you open your wallet and the only thing that flies out is dust? You use a scientific method taught to me by one of mentors called **CART**.

- **C**ancel every negative thought that comes into your head by saying out loud "CANCEL".

- **A**ffirm that you *are* successful and you *do* have a millionaire mind.

- **R**eplace *any* thoughts of shortage with thoughts of abundance.

- **T**alk to that money, call it and *command* it to come home to you.

Some might say that seems crazy – 'if I were to do that, I would sound like a nut'. I would rather act crazy and be rich than appear sane and only have beans to eat, how about you? I am not suggesting you do this in public, although I have. You can't control what others think about you, anyway. Besides, are any of those people going to come to your rescue when your car note is past due? Use this scientific method, and you will learn how to control your thoughts in the right direction when the conditions of your life are headed in the wrong direction.

What You See is What You Get

The power of vision is awesome. No, I am not talking about the vision that develops in your imagination or thinking processes, but the kind of vision that comes from those two round things in your head called eyeballs. What you physically see has a major impact on where you end up in life. Of course, this has a scientific reason behind it, also. When you see things, images, places or conditions over a period of time, you are actually building a kind of brain map or pathway in your brain that causes you to think and feel in those terms. This triggers you to take action to move toward those conditions and things. This works, both in moving you toward good things as well as bad things.

Let me share with you an interesting story. There is a famous ancient king by the name of David. The Bible says this man "was after God's own heart". Ever since the days of his youth, he was a dedicated worshiper of God. As an adult and king of ancient Israel, he walked and lived in utmost integrity. Nonetheless, in an instant, this honorable man not only committed adultery, but also murder.

What happened? Well, one day this goodly man went to his rooftop for some fresh air. As he was gazing at the sunset, lo and behold, he saw a beautiful woman taking a bath.

He shook his head, closed his eyes and looked away. Everything was fine…until the following day. He went out to his rooftop at the same time the next day, and he saw the same thing - Bathsheba taking a bath. What do you think he was thinking about that night when he went to bed? I guarantee he was not counting sheep!

It all started when he saw her bathing. Then, he began thinking about her bathing. Before long, his mind's eye saw her taking a bath and he was right there with her, smiling like a possum. Before you know it, this was no longer a dream in his head; it became a reality. That rascal was singing rub-a-dub-tub with another man's wife, and then he had her husband killed. Some say, he fell into temptation. If you ask me, he fell into more than just temptation; it's more like a set of bazooka's he fell into…head first! The truth is, because of the law that governs science, what he saw with his eyes impacted the neurons in his brain, setting off a chemical reaction which coursed through his system. That affected his emotions and thoughts, prompting his actions. That is the science of how the ancient king named David permitted himself to do the forbidden hokie-pokie with another man's wife! There you have it - what you see is what you get.

To help visualize what you want, find photos of those things, and post them where you can see them. As you look at them, they are drawing brain maps in your head that eventually your body will follow. If you are looking at things you don't have or don't want, you will find that is what you will always have. However, if you start looking only at what you *do* want, it is just a matter of time before you have exactly that – everything you want! God gave you this wonderful tool for success, use it! Use it to attract the wonderful things you want in life, not the negative things you don't want. Look at yourself in the mirror and ask, "Am I looking at success or failure"? Whatever it is that you are seeing is what you will have.

It is interesting to note that after his experience, David wrote in the Psalms "I will put no evil before my eyes". Oh, if only we could learn our lessons as well as that great man did. Whether it is your desire to own a certain car or a house, or to have great success or anything else, look at it until it creates emotion. The emotion will fuel and fire chemical reactions in your brain, which in turn will affect your feelings, prompting you to act toward that thing. It is not hocus pocus, but the science of your focus.

> *"The hardest thing about education is not learning something new...*
> *but unlearning something old"*
>
> - The Professor -

Patti McKenna

Editor's Note

When I accepted the "job" of editing "The Power of Mentorship for the 21st Century", I had the advantage of having previous experience with the subject of mentorship through one of the authors who contributed to this book. My editing services were recommended to Don Boyer through Gregory Scott Reid, better known to me as "Greg". Don and I already had something in common before I undertook this project – Greg has been a mentor, as well as a friend, to both of us.

After Don invited me into the pages of this book, he gave me the opportunity to read "The Power of Mentorship, Volume I". The insight and inspiration I gained motivated me, and I vowed to help Don deliver another high-quality book to his readers. I was fortunate to be able to participate in the portrayal of the messages from these outstanding authors, speakers, and mentors.

One of the benefits of being an editor is that I actually get to see the book while it is in progress. Unbeknownst to me, as each chapter unfolded, I was being swayed by the author's message. In less than a week, I found becoming a mentor of sorts myself. Another week flew by, and I realized that Don had not only invited me into his book, but also into his life. In that short time, we had established a camaraderie and a working relationship that I wish everyone has the pleasure to experience in their lifetime. It is indeed what separated this project from that word called "work".

I share this with you so you will know that Don Boyer, Greg Reid, and all of the contributing authors in this book are genuine and sincere. They not only deliver a message, they live it. It is truly their mission to help others succeed. Because of this book, the number of mentors in my life has grown; and I can proudly claim that Don Boyer is one of them. Embrace his message; and I'm certain that you, too, will discover that there is an amazing and electrifying power in mentorship.

Patti McKenna

Mentors hold the golden key to unleash your potential and unlock your future!

Learn How to Succeed From Those Who Already Have!

Look at what the top experts are saying about, "The Power of Mentorship"

"Without mentors you cannot grow. You cannot succeed. You cannot live a happy, successful and fulfilled life without mentors period!!!"

Charlie "Tremendous" Jones
Renowned National Speaker

"I highly recommend that you not only read "The Power of Mentorship," but read it again to fully appreciate the sincere, heartfelt messages of great wisdom shared by these talented, successful authors and you then will be truly inspired to take action to become all you were meant to be."

Jim Rohn
"America's Foremost Business Philosopher"

"In the end...the extent of our own success will be measured by the accomplishments we have helped create in others." What "The Power of Mentorship" has done, is bring together a mastermind of individuals that have opened up their hearts and vault of information and wish to pass these wisdoms on to you."

Gregory Scott Reid
The Millionaire Mentor

"From the beginning of time everything we have learned was taught to us by someone else. Mentors teach us the pathway to success. What you have done in this book, "The Power of Mentorship" is help pass the torch of success from one generation to the next."

William E. Bailey
Millionaire Extraordinaire
Winner of prestigious Horatio Alger Award

Mentorship is passing the torch of Success from one generation to the next.

In this new and exciting book "The Power of Mentorship" the authors give you an exclusive opportunity to sit in an inner circle and share the wealth of wisdom from some of the most experienced mentors of our day. Mentorship has become a lost art in the fast pace of the 21st century lifestyle. Yet it was the ancient form of training that produced some of the most powerful men and women in recorded history. From Kings and Queens to World Leaders, mentorship was the key element to their achievement.

Now is your chance to be mentored in

Leadership
Finances
Relationships
Health
Wisdom
Success
And much more!

Don Boyer

ORDER TODAY! **Call Toll Free (866) 871-4487** **Order online at AMAZON.com**

Quick Order Form

The Power of Mentorship
For the 21st Century
By Don Boyer
$12.95

Shipping: $2.50 for first book
$1.25 for each additional book
(California residents add 8.25% sales tax)

Fax Orders	Telephone Orders
Send this form to: 562-945-5457	Call Toll Free: 1-866-871-4487 (Have your credit card ready)
Email Orders melindatavera@realifeteaching.com	

Name_____

Address:_____

City/State/Zip:_____ _____

Phone: _____

Email: _____

Method of Payment: Visa or   Master Card

Card Number: _____

Name on Card: _____

Expiration Date: _____

3-digit security code on back of card: _____

(If billing address is different from shipping address, please provide.)

Zig Ziglar's Affirmation Cards
(cut and carry)

My Personal Commitment

I, _____, am serious about setting and reaching my goals in life, so on this _____ day of _____, 20__ I promise myself that I will take the first step toward setting those goals.

I am willing to exchange temporary pleasures in the pursuit of happiness and the striving for excellence in the pursuit of my goals. I am willing to discipline my physical and emotional appetites to reach the long-range goals of happiness and accomplishment. I recognize that to reach my goals I must grow personally and have the right mental attitude, so I promise to specifically increase my knowledge in my chosen field and regularly read positive growth books and magazines. I will also attend lectures and seminars, take courses in personal growth and development. I will utilize my time more effectively by enrolling in Automobile University and listening to motivational and educational recordings while driving or performing routine tasks at home or in the yard. I will keep a list of my activities including the completion dates for each project in my Goals Program. I further promise to list good ideas (mine and those of others) and to note thoughts, power-phrases, and quotations which have meaning to me.

_____

Date   Signature

A Life-Changing Procedure

The eyes are the windows of the soul. So, to the person you are capable of becoming, each evening, just before you go to bed, stand in front of a mirror alone and in the first-person, present-tense, look yourself in the eye and repeat with passion and enthusiasm paragraphs A, B, C, and D. Repeat this process every morning and every evening from this day forward. Within one week you will notice remarkable changes in your life. After thirty days, add the procedure at the bottom of this card.

A. "I, _____, am an honest, intelligent, organized, responsible, committed, teachable person who is sober, loyal, and clearly understands that regardless of who signs my paycheck, I am self-employed. I am an optimistic, punctual, enthusiastic, goal-setting, smart working, self-starter who is a disciplined, focused, dependable, persistent positive thinker with great self-control, and am an energetic and diligent team player and hard worker who appreciates the opportunity my company and the free enterprise system offer me. I am thrifty with my resources and apply common sense to my daily tasks. I take honest pride in my competence, appearance and manners, and am motivated to be and do my best so that my healthy self-image will remain on solid ground. These are the qualities which enable me to manage myself and help give me employment security in a no job-security world.

B. "I, _____, am a compassionate, respectful encourager who is a considerate, generous, gentle, patient, caring, sensitive, personable, attentive, fun-loving person. I am a supportive, giving, and forgiving, clean, kind, unselfish, affectionate, loving, family-oriented, human being; and I am a sincere and open-minded good listener and a good-finder who is trustworthy, these are the qualities which enable me to build good relationships with my associates, neighbor, mate and family.

C. "I _____, am a person of integrity, with the faith and wisdom to know what I should do and the courage and convictions to follow through. I have the vision to manage myself and to lead others. I am authoritative, confident, and humbly grateful for the opportunity life offers me. I am fair, flexible, resourceful, creative, knowledgeable, decisive and an extra-miler with a servant's attitude who communicates well with others. I am a consistent, pragmatic teacher with character and a finely-tuned sense of humor. I am an honorable person and am balanced in my personal, family and business life, and have a passion for being, doing and learning more today so I can be, do and have more tomorrow.

D. "These are the qualities of the winner I was born to be, and I am fully committed to developing these marvelous qualities with which I have been entrusted. Tonight I'm going to sleep wonderfully well. I will dream powerful, positive dreams, I will awaken energized and refreshed; tomorrow's going to be magnificent, and my future is unlimited. Recognizing, claiming and developing these qualities which I already have gives me a legitimate chance to be happier, healthier, more prosperous, more secure, have more friends, greater peace of mind, better family relationships and legitimate hope that the future will be even better."

Repeat the process the next morning and close by saying, "These are the qualities of the winner I was born to be, and I will develop and use these qualities to achieve my worthy objectives. Today is a brand new day and it's mine to use in a marvelously productive way."

After 30 days, add the next step:

Choose your strongest quality and the one you feel needs the most work. Example: Strongest -- honest. Needs most work – organized. On a separate 3x5, print "I _____, am a completely honest person, and every day I am getting better at being organized." Keep this 3x5 card handy and read it out loud at every opportunity for one week. Repeat this process with the second strongest quality and the second one which needs the most work. Do this until you've completed the entire list. Use this self-talk procedure as long as you want to get more of the things money will buy and all of the things money won't buy.

Note: Because of some painful experiences in the past (betrayal, abuse, etc.) there might be a word or two that brings back unpleasant memories (example: discipline). Eliminate the word or substitute another word.

Quick Order Form

The Power of Mentorship
For the 21st Century
By Don Boyer
$12.95

Shipping: $2.50 for first book
$1.25 for each additional book
(California residents add 8.25% sales tax)

Fax Orders	Telephone Orders
Send this form to: 562-945-5457	Call Toll Free: 1-866-871-4487 (Have your credit card ready)
Email Orders melindatavera@realifeteaching.com	

Name_____

Address:_____

City/State/Zip:_____

Phone: _____

Email: _____

Method of Payment: Visa   or   Master Card

Card Number: _____

Name on Card: _____

Expiration Date: _____

3-digit security code on back of card: _____

(If billing address is different from shipping address, please provide.)

Notes